ONE HUNDRED
WALKS IN THE
PEAK DISTRICT

ONE HUNDRED WALKS IN THE PEAK DISTRICT

Iain Grant

MAINSTREAM
PUBLISHING

EDINBURGH AND LONDON

ACKNOWLEDGMENTS

There are several people to whom I owe thanks: Paul and Gillie Sullivan for putting me up and putting up with me; Sandy Wilkie for doing the maps; Mum for lending me her motor-cycle; Dad for his many helpful comments and the initial inspiration; and Nikki for driving me around, spending so much time walking with me and being the ideal walking companion.

Copyright © Iain Grant, 1993
Maps by Sandy Wilkie

First published in Great Britain in 1993 by
MAINSTREAM PUBLISHING COMPANY (EDINBURGH) LTD
7 Albany Street
Edinburgh EH1 3UG

ISBN 1 85158 525 7

A catalogue record for this book is available from the British Library

Typeset in Palatino by Litho Link Ltd, Welshpool, Powys, Wales
Printed in Great Britain by The Cromwell Press, Melksham, Wiltshire

CONTENTS

THE PEAK DISTRICT

I have been walking in the Peak, off and on, for almost 20 years, ever since my Dad started dragging me kicking and screaming on to the hills on Sunday mornings, long weekends and odd days off, often when I fancied a lie-in. He introduced me to the Peak, and showed me many of its little nooks and crannies as I sullenly tagged along behind him. I must have spoiled many of his days out. Gradually, though, thanks to him I grew to love it and to know it well.

Even now, however, I am sometimes astonished by the variety of scenery one finds in the Peak and the marked contrast between the different types of landscape to be found within its borders. This is particularly vivid where the limestone of the White (or Low) Peak, in the south and centre, meets the gritstone of the Dark (or High) Peak in the north, and the moors of the east and west, but even without crossing those boundaries you can pass through several sorts of landscape in the course of a few hours' walk.

As a teenager, gloomy and morose and afflicted by dark thoughts about the futility of human existence, I used to love the wild, empty northern moors, Kinder and especially Bleaklow, whose name, I thought, summed up my life. Now I am older, happier and, I hope, wiser, I see the beauty of the limestone landscape – the richness of the wildlife, the wildflowers, the drama of the dales, the villages – though I still appreciate the harsher side of the Peak's largely uninhabited gritstone moors and high hills.

For the purpose of this book I have divided the Peak into six geographical sections: the walks in the South-East and South-West are mainly in limestone country, though the South-West ones dip an occasional toe into the gritstone of the western moors; West, North-West and North-East are all gritstone; the central region is predominantly limestone, though there is a distinctive line of hills here which are composed of shale and clay, and some of the walks also venture into the gritstone country to the north and east. There is something there for every taste and every mood.

THE WALKS

Most of these walks – 92 of them – are circular, starting and finishing in the same place. The final eight are ribbons – walks to somewhere from somewhere else. All of them involve some climbing (though there is at least one which I would have some reservation about calling a 'hill walk'). I have tried either to start the circular walks at a car park, or to provide information about parking nearby.

I have had to assume that people using this book will travel by car simply because the system of public transport in the Peak District (though to call it a 'system' is probably to over-dignify it somewhat) is atrocious, especially in the south – some of these walks make use of old railway lines and, whilst this makes for easy walking, it would be easier to get around if there were still trains running along them. Most of the towns and villages are visited by about two buses a day, except on special occasions – you can get to Bakewell, for instance, from almost anywhere on a Monday (market day), but the rest of the week only from Matlock with any degree of reliability.

The ribbon walks rely on public transport, making use of either trains or a regular bus service (which is why there are so few of them). They fall into two categories: those where transport is available back to the beginning (or to the starting point from the end), and those where the transport available is to some common point not on the route (usually Sheffield or Manchester). They do, however, need a certain amount of logistical planning before being undertaken – please consult the relevant timetables.

Obviously, there are rather more than 100 walks possible in the Peak District, and the selection given here, whilst I have tried to make it comprehensive, covering as much of the Peak's variety of geography as possible, is not meant to be anything like exhaustive of the Peak's potential for excellent walking.

My main criterion for including a walk has been that the route taken should be interesting: I always enjoy a variety of scenery rather than miles and miles of monotony, and if a visit to some point of interest can also be included, then so much the better. Some areas offer more potential for this than others, and if some areas seem more highly represented here, this is the reason.

There have been other important criteria. Ease of navigation was one – the route taken between individual points along a walk is, in some instances, not necessarily the most direct, but it is usually the easiest to find.

Another was crowd avoidance – tourism (along with quarrying and cheese making) is the Peak District's biggest earner, but it does mean that parts of it are thronged at certain times. I have tried, therefore, to include walks which are slightly off the beaten track. One of my worst moments on the hills was coming down Cave Dale after a long, satisfying trek, to find a party of 500 Young Christian Women of All Nations (mainly Americans) coming the other way. The noise was intolerable and I had to climb the dale side and sit, sullenly, at the top until they had passed. I have pointed out those areas which tend towards getting crowded (e.g. Castleton and Hartington) and given advice on when to steer clear of them.

I have also tried, for ease and convenience, to make sure that the walks fit on one map. I was greatly aided in this by the fact that the Ordnance Survey's Outdoor Leisure series maps are quite comprehensive (especially The White Peak). There are, however, some exceptions to this rule, and some of the walks in Bradwell, Langsett and Hathersage, and two of the ribbon walks, require more than one map.

Because of the law of trespass which pertains in England, I have also tried to confine the walks to established rights of way. There are one or two instances where I have been unable to establish whether the route I take is a right of way or not, but there has been no evidence in these cases to suggest that walkers are unwelcome.

In general, in the Peak, access is improving: new access agreements are being forged between the Park authorities and the landowners and little green signs denoting open access are springing up – a most welcome sight. Nevertheless, it has been a source of great irritation to me, not just in compiling the book but as a walker myself, that there are huge tracts of the Peak District to which I am denied access.

Readers will also notice that a great many pubs are mentioned in the text. One of the great pleasures of walking in the Peak is the number of fine hostelries which can be visited. Obviously, you should never walk when drunk, but there is nothing finer than a pint, or possibly two, en route, except for a pint, or possibly two, at the end of a walk. All the pubs mentioned by name in the text are known to me, sometimes intimately, and the recommendations contained therein are the result of many hours of arduous research.

EXPLANATORY NOTES

All the distances given in the text are approximate. There seems to me to be little point in saying that a walk is 8.8 miles long rather than that it is nine miles long as, for one thing, two people with pedometers walking the same route will produce different results anyway, and the precise length of a walk is affected by how many obstacles you have to avoid and so on. Similarly, where I say in the book that it is 350 yds from, say, a stile to a wood, this is meant as a rough guide and not a scientific measurement, being based only on my estimation of the distance by foot and eye. I cheerfully admit that one day's 350 yds could well be another's 400.

The time I advise allowing for each walk is based on the following considerations: an average walking speed of three miles per hour plus allowances for the amount of climbing involved and the difficulty of the terrain. This, again, is an approximate figure, though if I err here I have tried to make sure that I err on the side of caution.

Where I talk about the kind of 'going' to be expected, this refers to conditions underfoot (though, of course, these change enormously with the weather). As a rough guide: 'easy going' usually means walking on roads, old railways, lanes and clear, well-defined paths over level ground; 'moderate going' is footpaths, often indistinct, over rougher terrain; 'hard going' can mean bog-trotting over pathless peat hags or scrambling up steep hillsides. Where I talk about a mixture of two types of going (as in 'moderate and hard going'), the one given first is the predominant condition (just as the Mystery Voice in 20 Questions used to describe things as 'mainly animal with vegetable connections').

Where compass bearings are given (in those few walks involving traversing open country) these are according to grid north. The compass needle points to magnetic north, grid north being approximately six degrees east of this, so adjust the compass accordingly.

The maps in the book are not meant to be anything other than guides to where to look on the relevant Ordnance Survey maps.

Some other terms used in the text:

Track	broad path, not necessarily right of way
Lane	walled or enclosed track, sometimes metalled, not often open to traffic
Road	open to traffic, metalled

Open country	countryside to which there is open access, freedom to wander at will
N,S,E,W, etc.	rough direction of travel – exact direction given by compass bearings (grid N)
Clough	a steep-sided valley, usually smaller than a dale, and usually in the north of the Peak, though there are exceptions
Dale	a steep-sided valley, larger than a clough, and usually in limestone country

PREPARING TO WALK

There is no space here for an exhaustive guide to safety on the hills or the best equipment to use, but there are certain things which should always be borne in mind when getting ready to go hill walking.

CLOTHING AND EQUIPMENT

Always wear good, stout walking boots to support the ankles and prevent injury. They need to have soles which won't slip on smooth rock or wet grass. They also need to be waterproof – wet feet go soft and get blistered which, apart from being not at all pretty, is at best uncomfortable and at worst dangerous (if, for some reason, you have to get to civilisation quickly and can only manage a hobble). Two pairs of socks underneath these will also help prevent blisters by stopping friction between foot and boot.

Always have a waterproof jacket or cagoul. The actual getting wet is not the main problem; the getting cold which results from it is. You can also use this to keep the wind off. Waterproof over-trousers are also a boon.

Similarly, have sufficient clothing to keep yourself warm. This applies even in summer – I have been sweating in a T-shirt in Edale and freezing in a bitter wind four miles later on top of Kinder Scout in July. The weather is always an unpredictable beast, so be prepared.

In winter, a hat, preferably a balaclava, though unfashionable, is a must – ten per cent of body heat is lost through the head. Thermal underwear is also a great asset in cold weather, with the added bonus that some people find it incredibly sexy. Clothing should always be of an absorbent material so that it soaks up your sweat, so leave those Crimplene trousers and your Bri-Nylon vest at home.

Never go on to the hills without a map. Most of the walks in this book are covered by the Ordnance Survey's 1:25,000 Outdoor Leisure series maps 1 (The Dark Peak) and 24 (The White Peak). The 1:50,000 Landranger series sheet 110 (Sheffield and Huddersfield) covers the others. Harvey's of Doune, in Perthshire, also do an excellent series of Walker's Maps and their 1:40,000 Dark Peak South and Dark Peak North are also very useful.

None of the walks over the moors in the North-East and North-West sections should ever be attempted without a good compass (e.g. a

Silva) with directional arrow and bearings in degrees and, of course, knowing how to use it both to orient your map and to orient yourself. In fact, a compass is invaluable on all the walks. Knowing where you are going (e.g. in a fog) can, at the very least, save you time, and can be much more important than that.

It is also important to have with you a first-aid kit containing at least the following: sticking-plasters for cuts and blisters (chiropodist's felt also helps); a bandage and safety pin for strapping a turned ankle; anti-histamine cream for bites and stings (in summer); aspirin; salt or some very salty food (for cramp).

Also, carry a whistle on the moors, even though you will, I hope, never have to use it. The international distress signal is six short blasts over ten seconds, repeated every minute. You can also use a torch to signal in the same way.

Take fluid – a stout bottle of water will do, though some people prefer to take a flask of tea. Dehydration, especially in summer, is a serious problem. It is also advisable to take some food with you. You are probably not going to die for want of a sandwich on a day's outing, but you might feel ill. A cheese and pickle sandwich in a sheltered hollow is, in any case, one of the great pleasures of being on the hills.

OTHER TIPS

The ideal size, in terms of safety, for a party of hill walkers, is four. In the event of an accident or injury, one person can then remain with the injured party whilst the other two go to get help.

Always keep the party together. Walking pace should be adjusted to suit the slowest member. Also, rest every hour. Sitting down for five minutes restores tired legs. When you do sit down, put on an extra layer of clothing to conserve body heat.

Leave a note of your route with somebody who is not going on the walk so that, should you fail to reappear, they can contact the authorities and get you rescued. (Let them know if your non-appearance is simply due to a change of plan.)

Never walk when feeling ill. If you or a member of your party becomes seriously fatigued en route, get down off the hill and return to base as quickly as possible.

Always keep an eye on the weather, and amend your route accordingly. Don't try to navigate across country without a compass in a fog, get off the hills if it starts to snow heavily. If caught in the open in a thunderstorm, get down off the tops. The best position to be in is lying flat on the ground – never stand beneath a tree or in the mouth of a cave.

Allow yourself enough time to do the walk and get back safely before dark. A small torch will help if you have to read maps in the dark.

Some of the walks in this book involve walking short distances along roads. When doing so, keep to the right, facing the oncoming traffic, and take extra care on bends.

This is just a matter of personal taste, but I always like to take with me a pocket guide to wild flowers. You might also like to consider one for birds and a small pair of binoculars.

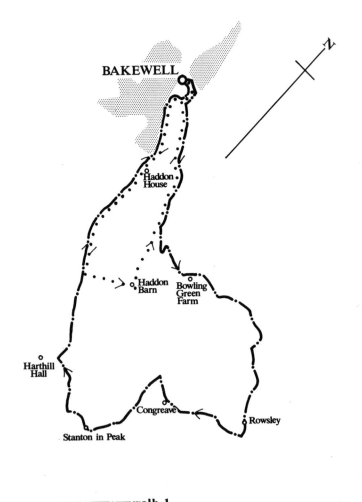

BAKEWELL

Haddon
House

Haddon
Barn

Bowling
Green
Farm

Harthill
Hall

Congreave

Rowsley

Stanton in Peak

●—·—●—·—●—·— walk 1
· · · · · · · · · · · walk 2

0   1 mile

THE SOUTH-EAST

BAKEWELL

The capital of the Peak. Well, the largest town in the national park, anyway, famed for its puddings and tarts (confectionery items, not inhabitants). Despite this, the town is one of the best: it's quaint and pretty, it's set in rolling countryside and it has at least two excellent pubs (try the Red Lion and the Peacock). Monday is market day, when you can expect the town to be crowded and when you can also get there by public transport from as far away as Castleton.

WALK 1: Bakewell-Rowsley-Stanton-Shining Bank

A walk which takes you along the bank of the River Wye and through the Haddon Hall Estate, through woods and over gentle rolling hills.

Easy going, small climbs.
9½ miles, 3½ hrs.
Start SK217685.

From the square in Bakewell, take the Sheffield road to the NE, past the Red Lion and the Tourist Information office. Go over the bridge and take the first road off to the right. Three hundred yards along this there is a car park on the right, at the bottom of which is a footpath on the left going over the show ground.

This heads roughly SE, keeping close to the river, for just over a mile, until it meets a lane. Take this left, uphill, following it as it winds around the butt end of the old Buxton-Bakewell railway, after which it heads E for 400 yds before turning left, uphill once more, past a farm.

The lane bends round E again, coming to a junction 300 yds later. Take the lane on the left, heading E into the woods, on the other side of which, turn right on another lane, heading S, downhill into Rowsley.

When you come out on to the main road past the church, the post office and the Peacock, take the road opposite and to the left, signposted to Stanton in Peak.

Coming out of Rowsley to the S, the road leaves the houses, crosses the Wye and bends right, by the riverside. Follow it a further 300 yds and then, where it bends left uphill, cross the stile which leads to a footpath going straight on.

After 75 yds this path bends left and starts climbing uphill slightly. When you come to a wall, keep to the right of it, heading roughly SW, and then make for the right-hand corner of the small wood you see in front of you.

Here the path bends right and heads W to the road at Congreave. Turn right here (on an incredibly tight bend, so be careful) and head downhill for 300 yds. Then take the footpath on the left signposted to Stanton in Peak. As you climb the hill you can look back on to the estates of both Chatsworth and Haddon Hall. This is the time to start singing *The Red Flag*. (Ironically.)

You emerge in Stanton conveniently close to the Flying Childers (a pub. Named after a racehorse. Red Rum). Turn right on the road and follow it out of the village, bending left. After some 500 yds you will come to a small crossroads and a footpath, which you should take to the right, as it leads diagonally over a field to a lane. Turn left here, and follow the lane downhill until it comes to a serious right-hand bend after 250 yds, where the footpath carries straight on.

The path brings you downhill on to the B5056, which can get quite busy at times. Turn right on the road, past the turning on your left to Youlgreave and, 150 yds later, take the footpath on the left past the quarry. It takes you uphill through some woods. Keep to the left of the wall as you emerge from the woods – the path is well marked and easy to follow – and continue roughly NW over this broad, rolling hillside for three-quarters of a mile until a stile near the top right corner of a field takes you off to the right slightly, turning N and going downhill to meet a lane taking you to the main road just to the left of Haddon House Farm.

There is a footpath on the other side of the road which goes between the houses, over the playing field and by the side of the river and back into the very centre of Bakewell.

WALK 2: Bakewell and Wye Valley

A short, pleasant riverside stroll, with no great effort involved.

Easy going, one small climb.
3 miles, 1 hr.
Start SK217685.

From the bridge over the Wye, take the walk on the S (right) side of the river. Cross the playing field and follow the narrow lane between the houses on the other side. This will bring you to the main A6 road on the outskirts of the town.

Cross the road and take the signposted footpath. Just past the farm on your left, cross the stile and take the footpath on the left, through a wood. Follow this S, crossing the small footbridge at the bottom of Wigger Dale.

At the second stile after this, turn left and then left again at the second wall you come to. This will lead you downhill to the main road, past the car park for Haddon Hall.

Turn left on the main road for 250 yds, taking the footpath on the right, which is signposted, but the signpost is often hidden by the hedge. This crosses the river and winds through a wood for a few hundred yards, until it comes to a T-junction with a lane. Turn right here, then almost immediately left, following the river for a mile back to Bakewell.

When you have passed the show ground, cross the river via the footbridge on your left, turn right and go back the way you started out.

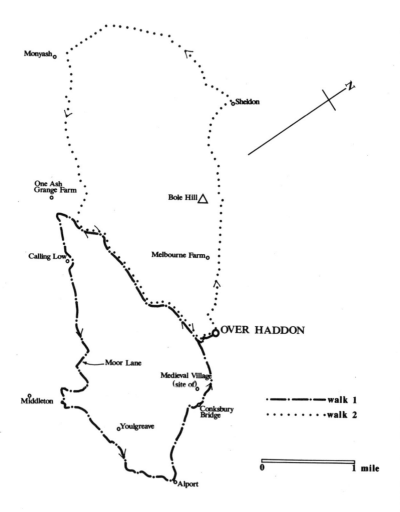

LATHKILL DALE

One of the most spectacular of all the Derbyshire dales, Lathkill Dale makes for superb walking, once you've found Over Haddon by following the road signs – no easy feat. Even finding the car park once you've found Over Haddon can be a bit tricky. Lathkill Dale is a fine place for a gentle walk in most seasons, though it can look extremely desolate in winter, and the scars left by the lead mining which took place there until the end of the 19th century are sufficiently healed to lend the place an air of romance. You will come across ruins and workings burrowed into the daleside at practically every turn.

WALK 1: Over Haddon-Cales Dale-Bradford Dale-Alport

A sort of compare and contrast exercise between two dales: Lathkill, rugged and beautiful, and Bradford, gentle and charming, including a hike over the limestone plateau.

Easy going with two stiff climbs.
9 miles, 4 hrs.
Start SK203665.

Turn right as you come out of the car park, and head down the very steep hill, following the lane which the locals have called, wittily, Steep Lane. Pass the signs facing downhill which indicate a 30-mile-an-hour speed limit and wonder how any vehicle could achieve more than a crawl up here.

You will come to the end of the road at a house called Lathkill Lodge which may well have Range Rovers parked outside it. Turn right here, through a wooden gate and on to the Lathkill Dale footpath. If you are on the right path you will notice a notice nailed to a tree on your left which says that access along the footpath is free except on the Thursday of Easter Week, when you have to pay a toll. Luckily, you will reflect, it isn't the Thursday of Easter week (unless, of course, it is, in which case, bad luck).

Follow the path along the dale bottom for about two miles, until you come to a wooden footbridge across the River Lathkill where it bends right and another small dale joins from the left. If it's that time of day, it's a good idea to have your sandwiches here, as it's a beautiful spot and very sheltered, and the scenery opens out once you come out of the dale – there isn't another sandwich spot for three or four miles.

Having cheesed and pickled, cross the footbridge and follow the path for about 100 yds, until it divides, and then take the lower path, on the left. When you've crossed the second stream you won't be able to help noticing the big hill in front of you. You've got to get up it.

At the top of the steep bit there's a stile to have a sit on and a wall to lean against. Cross over, and follow the path over the fields. Whilst doing this it is worth peeking to your left at the lip of Lathkill Dale, an impressive gash in the otherwise uninterrupted landscape.

Continue across now open countryside until you come to a road. The path comes out at a fork, and you should take the upper branch, leading away to the left.

In a short while you will come to a car park on your right, and notice ruefully that it is cheaper to park here than in Over Haddon. To the left of the car park, take the lane over the moor, called Moor Lane. It is festooned with notices telling you not to fall down any of the disused mineshafts this area is dotted with. Good idea.

Soon the path turns to the left and begins the descent into Youlgreave – a pretty village, but you're not going there, you're heading for Bradford Dale. So, when the path comes out on to the road, you are going to take the one opposite, over the little bit of woodland, to the road you can see at the bottom of the hill. At the end of this, turn right and follow the road past some large and impressive houses.

When, after a few hundred yards, the road bends left, there will be a footpath on the left, running down the right-hand side of a little dale. Take this and descend into Bradford Dale, pausing as the path winds down the hillside to admire the beauty of the scene, especially, aah, that little bridge in front of you.

Cross over the little bridge and turn left. Bradford Dale is stuffed with water birds, and others, and any ornithologist will have a fine time with the little grebes, dippers, different types of wagtail and what have you. The big woolly ones that go 'baa' are sheep.

You will come, eventually, to the waterfront bits of Youlgreave and Bradford and have a road to cross. Keep following the river bank (you may have to cross the stream briefly, but cross back again immediately).

Just before you come into the next village, Alport, there is a remarkable rock formation on your right – about 100 feet high, it appears to be cracked from bottom to top. If you have a walking stick, it might be fun to try to prise the two sides apart.

In the village, cross over the main road and head up the green sward that is the foot of Lathkill Dale. There are one or two places where the path seems to disappear here, but as long as you remember to keep the river and the fence to your right, you can't go wrong.

You will pass by the windows of Raper Lodge, where the famous but not very good film adaptation of D H Lawrence's *The Virgin and the Gypsy* was made. Contain your excitement and keep going straight ahead, climbing a little, until you reach the end of the path at the medieval Conksbury Village. There is nothing there now beyond a series of lumps on the hillside but, with a bit of imagination and if you screw your eyes up, you can just about make out where the houses were.

Much more impressive is the medieval Conksbury Bridge, down the hill on the right. It has been improved and strengthened, but it retains most of its character and looks as if it could be in one of those medieval towns in the south of France rather than the middle of Derbyshire. Cross the bridge and turn left through a gate immediately after on to the path which will lead you back to Lathkill Lodge. Turn right and struggle up the hill back to the car park. The Lathkill Hotel in the village, it is interesting to note at this point, does an excellent pint of Ward's Bitter.

WALK 2: Over Haddon-Sheldon-Monyash

An upland walk skirting the two very different villages of Sheldon and Monyash, ending in a glorious descent into Lathkill Dale.

Moderate going, easy climbs.
10 miles, 4 hrs.
Start SK203665.

Turn left out of the car park on to main road. Less than 100 yds on the right there's a stone-built barn with a stile next to it. Cross the stile and head uphill over the fields, bending left after the first wall.

Cross over the next main road (B5055) and continue along the footpath opposite and to the right, aiming for the gap in the wall by a small barn. Continue for three-quarters of a mile until the footpath descends to meet another road in Kirk Dale. Here turn right around the bend a little and take the first left, a cart track which will bring you to Sheldon.

Emerging in the village (quaint but dull – the phone box is the only social amenity), turn left on main road. Follow this road as it bends left out of the village for 700 yds then, just before a farm to your left, take the footpath on the right signposted to Flagg.

This brings you out on to a long, straight stretch of road where there are sometimes cars parked but there is never anyone about. Turn right and 100 yds later take the footpath on the left over the hill strangely named High Low.

This brings you to the edge of Monyash, and when you emerge on to the road there is a footpath opposite signposted to Lathkill Dale. Take this unless you fancy a pint in the Bull's Head, in which case turn right into the village and then left.

The path is easy to follow, sticking to the bottom of Bagshaw Dale, and when you reach the main road on the other side of Monyash, the path you want is opposite and to your left. Follow it down and into the dale bottom and it brings you back to Over Haddon.

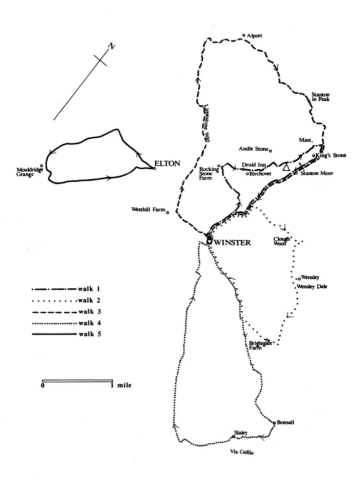

WINSTER

A charming little town well worth exploring in its own right – especially during its wakes, which are held early every summer. Parking your car in the village is a bit of a problem – there is no designated car park as such, but there are infrequently used roads with no houses, such as the top of East Bank (conveniently close to the wonderful Miner's Standard pub and the B5056) where a car can be left with no trouble.

WALK 1: Winster-Birchover-Stanton Moor

A superb variety of scenery is to be experienced on this short walk through farmland, woods and over Stanton Moor – littered with prehistoric artefacts and a small stone circle. A compass would come in quite handy on Stanton Moor.

Moderate going, some climbing.
5½ miles, 2½ hrs.
Start SK242606.

At the E end of high street take the footpath N, signposted to Birchover, down a narrow alley opposite an antique shop. As you leave the houses you can see the path carved into and winding up the bank opposite, coming out to the left of a farm perched on top.

This brings you out on to a track. Turn left round the farm until you come to a minor road, where turn left past the cottages opposite then quickly right on the footpath by the right of Birchover Wood. If the weather is clear enough you can see Robin Hood's Stride from here ahead of you and to the right.

Follow the side of the wood until you come to the impossibly pretty Rocking Stone Farm, and turn right over the stile and down the lane in front of the farm. Where the lane bends left, use the stile in front of you and go down the hill to meet the lane at the bottom.

Turn right into the village. Emerging on to the road, turn left to find yourself outside or possibly (who knows?) inside the Druid Inn. Opposite the Druid there's a track leading to the right uphill. Take it, skirting the village through Dungeon Wood.

This brings you to the main road. Just before you get there, there are magnificent views behind you to Youlgreave and Bradford Dale. What a shame you're facing the wrong way.

Turn left on to the main road, past a stone-cutting company for 500 yds. Just as the woods on the left side of the road come to an end and there's an open field (with the Andle Stone in it) take the footpath on the right past a huge pile of boulders put there to stop people driving on to the moor.

A few hundred yards uphill there's a large (natural) standing stone with rungs (unnatural) in it. Take the path on the left, along the edge of the moor.

Soon you will come to a gate into a plantation, which you should enter. Unusually for such things, this is a plantation of birch trees, probably the species which would grow here naturally, so it is actually quite pleasant and, what is more, teeming with wildlife. It certainly makes a change from the miles and miles of regimented pine one is used to encountering on hill tops.

Before entering the wood you will have been able to see a radio mast, and you will catch the occasional glimpse of it now – it is this you are making for. Because this is a working plantation containing active quarries, the landscape here changes constantly so the paths tend to disappear, making navigation trickier (though, of course, more exciting). Make, therefore, for the mast – there is a track leading right up to it – and, finding yourself directly S of it, head as nearly due E as you can.

You should come soon to a track on the other side of the plantation. When you do, turn right (S), taking you past the Nine Ladies stone circle and out of the woods. There are now spectacular views to your left. Unfortunately, they are largely views of Matlock, but you can't have everything. Soon Winster heaves into view, too, on the hill in front of you.

Coming down off the moor you find yourself on a minor road. Turn right and then take the footpath almost immediately on the left. This path goes due S, past a farm, until it comes to the lip of the bank which you climbed on your way out of Winster. From here you should be able to see the way back – downhill, bending slightly right into the trees and back on to the path leading up the alleyway to the high street.

WALK 2: Winster-Clough Wood-Wensley-Brightgate

Again, there's a huge variety of scenery within this short walk which takes you through old woodland and up on to Bonsall Moor.

Moderate going with climbing.
6 miles, 2½ hrs.
Start SK242606.

Leave Winster heading N on the same path as for Walk 1, bringing you to the track by Ivy House. Turn right here and follow the track for 700 yds.

When you see a gate on your left, there is an easy-to-miss low stone stile set into the wall on the right. This is the start of the path which leads you down the clough and over the stile into Clough Wood.

Follow the path as it leads you way downhill across the bottom of the clough and out of the woods, by which time you should be walking due E. When you emerge into the open there is a peculiar stone arch set into the hillside just ahead of you, and a path leading up the hill below you. Go down to meet this path and take it almost to the very bottom of the hill. Where this path splits into three, take the middle path, which is waymarked, over the bottom of the clough and into the woods on the other side.

There is quite a climb now, up through Cambridge Woods and down into the hamlet of Wensley. The circular pools and depressions you can see all over this area are old lead-mining shafts – this was the major region for lead production in the whole country for centuries, though the mines had a tendency to flood, hence some of the pools.

Turn left on to the main road in Wensley, and follow it round a right-hand bend past the Methodist chapel on your left. Shortly you come to a footpath on the right, which is signposted, leading through the houses and down into Wensley Dale.

Not, not *the* Wensley Dale, another one. Pleasant enough in its own way, though. In the dale bottom, take the track leading up the opposite side to your left. There is another climb now, and quite a long one, to a wall at the top of the hill.

You need to be able to see the stone-built farmhouse in a dip to the west (your right), a working quarry to the right of that (almost behind you) and a minor road in front of you at the very top of the hill. When you can, and you are standing at the narrowest side of a large sloping field, turn right (W) and follow the wall as it goes slightly downhill along the ridge to meet the road.

Once on the road, turn right and walk for 500 yds. Just before a roofless barn on your left, take the signposted footpath on the right which, if you take care not to fall down any of the mineshafts on the side of the hill, will bring you back to Winster.

WALK 3: Winster-Youlgreave-Stanton

Limestone moor, wooded dale and riverbank, a steep-streeted village and a gritstone moor – who could ask for more variety?

Moderate going, some climbing.
8 miles, 3 hrs.
Start SK242606.

Take the waymarked footpath leading W from the bottom (N end) of West Bank in Winster by the noticeboard for St John the Baptist church. This takes you into some woods near the excellently named Oddo House, crosses the B-road and comes to a T-junction with a lane.

Turn right here for 500 yds, until you come to the Elton road. Cross this and take the road opposite, signposted as the Limestone Way, for 700 yds downhill.

Just where it bends sharply right to meet the road, take the footpath straight ahead, bending left uphill, past the woods and bringing you to Robin Hood's Stride – a gritstone outcrop in this predominantly limestone landscape. It's 22 yds from the tall bit on the left to the tall bit on the right and, strangely enough, exactly the same distance the other way, so you could ask yourself, Erik von Daniken-style, whether this is a cricket pitch built by super-beings from outer space. The answer to this question, by the way, is 'no, it isn't'.

Carry on past the rocks and over a minor road. Pass to the left of a farm descending, almost a mile later, into Youlgreave. You should come out on to the road into the village from Gratton, turning right and crossing the bridge over the River Bradford. Take the footpath on the right immediately after. It crosses the river again very shortly, and then sticks more or less by the bank all the way to Alport, half a mile away.

Here the path crosses the river and comes out on to the main road by the bus stop. Turn right and take the first right down into the hamlet. Follow this street as it winds left through the houses, and then cross the bridge on the right at the back of the village.

The road climbs and twists for 100 yds and, just as you come to one of the most serious right-hand bends anywhere in the universe, there is a track on the left to the right of a house. Take this – it brings you back out on to the road after about 500 yds but it cuts out the corner and is much more pleasant.

Turn left on to the road, and cut out the next corner by taking the footpath on the right 150 yds later, bringing you out on to the Youlgreave-Winster road which can get (comparatively) busy, so be careful.

Just opposite and to the left is a road signposted to Stanton in Peak. Follow this through the village, past the Flying Childers, and now following the signs for Stanton Lees. This means you take the right fork in the centre of the village and carry straight on 200 yds later when the main road bends right.

After another 300 yds take the footpath on the right on to Stanton Moor, following the signs for the Nine Ladies Circle and, once past it, heading SSW to the road at the other side of the moor one mile later.

Turn right on to the road, then take the footpath immediately on the left, keeping left of the farm. This path heads due S over a half-metalled lane and carries on in the same direction for one more field, past a ramshackle barn to the right, until it reaches the brink of the bank of the valley separating it from Winster. Here it veers right somewhat, and the paths (or lack thereof) on the ground get a bit confusing. As a guideline, head just left of the church and the road running uphill at the right-hand side of the village.

Climbing up the opposite bank, look for a gate bearing a notice asking you to keep your dog on a lead which will lead you into a long, thin strip of pasture on the other side of the very scrubby bit of woodland growing at the bottom of the valley. This will bring you to a narrow alley leading on to Winster High Street, yards around the corner from where you left the village.

WALK 4: Winster-Bonsall-Slaley-Whitelow

Most of the distance covered is over limestone moor, but this walk also drops in on the bustling and very attractive little market town of Bonsall and the ash woods of the Via Gellia.

Moderate going with two climbs.
8 miles, 3 hrs.
Start SK242606.

From the High Street in Winster turn up past the old Market House (worth a look if it happens to be open) and the Bowling Green Inn, turning left at the top of the road. Where this street meets another, take the footpath on the left climbing up on to the moor.

The path climbs gently for about a mile, coming out on to Bonsall Lane which runs along the brow of the hill, and the continuation of the path is opposite and slightly to the left.

The only complicated bit of jiggery-pokery on this bit of the walk is where the path meets the corner of a lane: turn left on to it and then almost immediately right, bending diagonally away from the lane after one field.

As you come down off the moor near Bonsall – you will be able to see bits of the town strung out below you – you will come to a field which is more open than the previous ones and the wall you have been following comes to an abrupt end. Bend right here, going parallel to the road you can see to your left and making for the right-hand end of the road you can see in front of you.

This brings you out on to a corner in Bonsall Upper Town. As much as possible, carry on in the same direction by turning right then immediately left, past Chestnut Farm and Holly's Farm Shop.

At the other end of this short street, take the footpath which is slightly to the left but carries on in the same direction. This takes you down into Bonsall's Market Square, coming out opposite the King's Head and the medieval market cross. Here turn right along High Street.

When you come to another market cross at a junction with some toilets on the right-hand turning (The Dale), the path to Slaley goes off from the corner ahead of you, winding up the hill by the side of a wholesale car dealer.

Coming down into Slaley, turn left on to the road, following it downhill and to the right into the hamlet, past the modern bungalows. After 300 yds, take the footpath on the left downhill, near the entrance to Sunnyside Farm, the last building on the left.

This takes you down into the woods on the road kown as the Via Gellia – sounds Roman but it's named after the local Gell family who built it in the early 19th century. You descend almost to the road before, three-quarters of a mile from Slaley and deep in the woods, meeting a track which runs down the bottom of a clough. Take this to the right uphill and up on to Bonsall Moor, though there is a possible detour here – if you turn left and go down to the road (crossing carefully) it is possible to visit the Middleton Wood Caves, the source of a highly prized type of marble.

Keeping to the path over Bonsall Moor for two miles – it's easy to follow and heads in a straight line NW practically the whole way – brings you back out on to Bonsall Lane at the back of Winster. Turn left and take the footpath on the right 150 yds later, which takes you back to the village.

WALK 5: Elton-Gratton Dale

An interesting short walk up a dry dale which has been left pretty much to its own devices – it is wooded and scrubby and often full of birdsong. This is followed by an easy jog across moorland back to the starting point.

Moderate going with one climb.
3½ miles, 1½ hrs.
Start SK224609.

At the west end of Elton there's a corner where the road bends round to the right, splitting into two. Take the footpath here which continues along the line of the road through the village – it is signposted – to the right of Oddo House Farm.

After some 500 yds, the path begins to descend sharply, coming out in the bottom of Gratton Dale. As there is no right of way across the wall at the bottom of the dale to the footpath on the other side, technically what you have to do here is follow the track around the right-hand side of the farmhouse at the dale end on to the road, turn left and then left again at the phone box on to the dale path.

Once safely on to this path the walk is simplicity itself. Follow the dale until it stops. Don't turn right where Long Dale and Gratton Dale meet, but climb up the dale head, keeping left of the farm you can see perched on top of the hill, and follow the wall around to the road.

At the road turn left and, 250 yds later, take the signposted footpath on the left across the moor, heading NE and eventually dropping down on to a track and back to Elton.

Conies Dale (Peak Forest)

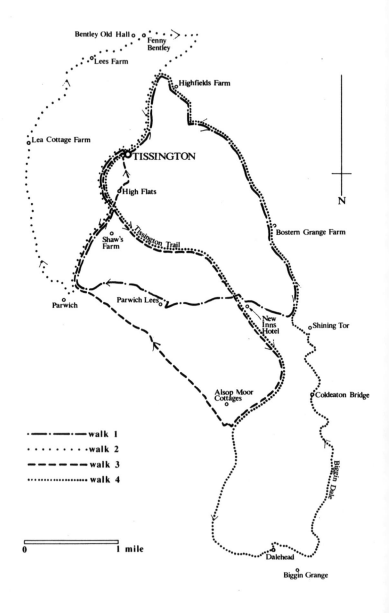

Bentley Old Hall
Fenny Bentley
Lees Farm
Highfields Farm
Lea Cottage Farm
TISSINGTON
High Flats
Bostern Grange Farm
Tissington Trail
Shaw's Farm
Parwich Lees
New Inns Hotel
Shining Tor
Parwich
Alsop Moor Cottages
Coldeaton Bridge
N

— · — · — walk 1
· · · · · · · walk 2
— — — walk 3
················· walk 4

0   1 mile

Biggin Dale

Dalehead
Biggin Grange

TISSINGTON

Tissington is a beautiful little village about as far south as you can go in the Peak District, and worth exploring in its own right. It is stuffed with history – its imposing 17th-century hall, a siegework left over from the English Civil War, even the gates on the main road into the village from the A515. Tragically, though, it remains publess, a factor which diminishes its attractions for many walkers. It is also, as you would probably guess from its name, on the Tissington Trail, the old Ashbourne-Buxton railway closed by Beeching in the early 1960s, which all of these walks utilise to some degree. It is interesting to walk in its own right, though it is heavily cycled at weekends, and because it is so easy you can use it to get a long way before turning and heading back by another route. All walks start from the trail car park in the village.

WALK 1: Tissington-Shining Tor (Mill Dale)-Parwich

A deceptively hilly walk showing the tremendous variety in the landscape of the White Peak within a few short miles. The walk follows a disused railway, peeps into Dovedale from the limestone plateau, takes a look along Mill Dale and crosses upland and lowland farming country.

Easy going with climbing.
9 miles, 4 hrs.
Start SK178521.

Take the trail S out of the car park (signposted Ashbourne). Shortly after it crosses the A515 main road the trail itself passes under a bridge. Immediately before this, climb up to the right on the path signposted to Dovedale, turning right on the track at the top, and continue through the caravan park at Highfields Farm.

This path brings you to a minor road. Turn right on to it and follow it until it bends right at a stone-built barn. The footpath goes off to the left here, uphill. Cross the minor road running along the brow of the hill on to the footpath opposite, going down into the hollow and bending off to the right.

After a bit more climbing and about four fields, you pass an impressive square limekiln to your left. Carry straight on past a junction with another path. Suddenly, after another quarter mile, there's a rocky outcrop; you bend slightly to the right and a view down into Dovedale opens out to your left.

Take the track to the right of the red-roofed Bostern Grange Farm and go through the gate on the other side, though when the track bends left carry straight on over the stile. Presently, there's a signpost to Milldale pointing left. Do as it commands.

Four hundred yards later you come to a crossroads, or crosspaths, to be accurate, with signs pointing to Milldale, Alsop en le Dale, Tissington and down past Hanson Grange into Dovedale. Typically, we don't want any of these.*

Aim halfway in between the Alsop and Milldale paths, i.e. bending slightly to the right and crossing the paddock diagonally uphill, and you will find a gate-stile through the wall. On the other side head straight downhill towards the gully you can see at the bottom.

Go to the right of the gully, following the wall, which will bring you to a road. Turn right and follow the road to its junction with the A515. Turn right again. You now have to walk along the main road for 150 yds, and it is not a pleasant experience as the traffic comes over a hill towards you and it never goes at less than 70 mph. The best thing to do is keep in as close to the right-hand verge as possible.

At the brow of the hill, take the footpath on the left, which passes down underneath the Tissington Trail,** bend half right and make for the copse you can see ahead of you. Passing right of this copse, aim for the right of the larger one downhill and continue on this line for half a mile along a grassy bank until you meet the Alsop-Parwich road.

On reaching the road, turn right immediately, almost back on yourself, and head along the overgrown lane leading away from the road at right angles. After 150 yds, go through the small rusty iron gate up the bank to the left. This path brings you round in front of Parwich Lees, a charming old farmhouse perched on the bank overlooking Bletch Brook.

This path continues for some way without losing any height before dropping down left into Parwich. Turn right into the village and, after passing the Methodist chapel on your left, the road bends round left. Here take the footpath on the right, down by the side of the drive into a cottage, signposted to Tissington two miles.

This path climbs out of the village, drops down over Bletch Brook and climbs again, eventually coming to a bridge over the Tissington Trail. Here you have a choice of routes – either drop down left on to the trail and follow it back to the car park, or carry straight on down the track, turning left at the bottom to explore the village.

*For the adventurous, a worthwhile but strenuous detour. Take the path off to the left, past the farm and down into the woods on the east slope of Dovedale. This will bring you to the valley bottom by Dove Hole (a cave). Having peeped into it and reached the dale bottom, turn right and make for Milldale but, before the footbridge, turn right uphill on the footpath signposted to Shining Tor. This rejoins the original route at the gully you skirt on top of the Tor.

**You can shorten the walk here by going under the bridge, turning right up on to the trail and taking it back to Tissington.

WALK 2: Tissington-Parwich-Fenny Bentley

This is a walk over gently rolling hills rather than anything truly dramatic. It is, however, not without its charm. In particular, the three villages visited en route all have features of interest, and the medieval manor house at Fenny Bentley is well worth seeing. In spring and early summer, furthermore, the area abounds with wild flowers.

Easy going with little climbing.
7 miles, 2½ hrs.
Start SK178521.

Take the Tissington Trail N from the car park and, after half a mile, turn right at the bridge and on to the path to Parwich. Coming down the hill into the village, make for the spire of the church, emerging just to the right of the village green and the Sycamore Inn.

Turn right on this road, past some modern houses on the right and out of the village. You should pass a small playing field on your right, at the far side of which is a footpath on the right signposted to Lea Hall. This path has not always been brilliantly maintained, but the more people use it, the better it will be.

Make your way alongside the brook and by a small pumping station to a track, turn right almost up to the gates of the sewage works, and then follow the track to the left. This track gets very boggy, but is passable, and brings you to a farm. Go through the gate on the other side, and then through a rickety wooden one, then heading diagonally left through a metal gate.

At the (diagonally) opposite corner of this field there's a footbridge over a stream. Now, if you keep to the left of the trees in front of you, following the path should be plain sailing. It will bring you to a minor road. Take the footpath on the other side down by the farm buildings, and take the track which goes sloping away uphill to the right on the other side of the farm.

When the track finishes abruptly, head for the right-hand side of the trees, where there's a gate. Go through it and the single gate on the right. Cross the brook via the stepping stones, and on the other side strike uphill to the left, heading for the next clump of trees. Follow the path leading through the trees, down and to the right, squishily over the brook and over the next brow.

This brings you to Woodeaves Farm. Go into the farmyard but keep to the left, going out of it on the track on the far side which leads away to the left and downhill.

Where this track starts to bend seriously downhill towards some houses there's a stile in the fence. Cross this and strike slightly uphill towards a gate and stile in the fence running downhill. This path takes you into Fenny Bentley.

As you arrive in the village, note the extraordinary building to your left – Cherry Orchard Farm, which incorporates much of the medieval Bentley Old Hall.

At this point the Coach and Horses lies 200 yds to your left, but you need to turn right up the main road and then left on the opposite side up Ashes Lane, past the church and into the village proper.

At the end of the houses take the footpath on the right signposted to Thorpe 1 mile, climbing over the brow of the hill and up the next to meet the Tissington Trail. Turn right here and this brings you back right to the car park.

WALK 3: Tissington-Alsop Moor-Parwich

Similar in route to Walk 1, this simple walk takes you further (and faster) on the Tissington Trail, climbing very gradually for some three miles before descending over some beautiful limestone countryside and then into Parwich, finally making its way back to Tissington.

Easy going, some climbing.
8 miles, 3 hrs.
Start SK178521.

Head N out of the car park on the Tissington Trail. Follow it as it bends first E and then W, for a while running parallel to and then crossing underneath the A515.

It now starts to bend E once more, again coming close to the main road but now above it and to the left. Where it crosses a minor road make your way down to the road, turning right to meet the main road. Here turn left and after 50 yds take the footpath on the right over a stile.

This footpath climbs a little but then descends more or less all the way to Parwich through Eaton Dale, and is very easy to follow, heading more or less SE all the way with no major turnings or obstacles.

Coming out on to the road, turn left into Parwich (about 500 yds) and, once into the village, pass the Methodist chapel on your left. When the road starts to bend left, take the footpath on the right, signposted to Tissington which, again, is easy to follow as it does not deviate much from its SSW course and there are no major obstacles.

When you have crossed over the first hill and squelched your way over Bletch Brook, the footpath heads left of the farm you can see on the other side of the hill and joins a track crossing a bridge over the Trail.

Cross the bridge and continue along the lane past a house on your right and into Tissington via the footpath on the left just after the lane bends right.

WALK 4: Tissington-Biggin Dale-Mill Dale

A long walk, so only for the very fit, but as long walks in the Peak go this one is quite easy, utilising the Tissington Trail to get a long way north and then returning through some of Derbyshire's most spectacular scenery.

Easy going with one difficult climb.
15 miles, 7 hrs.
Start SK178521.

Head N out of the car park on the Trail for about five miles. After it crosses underneath the main road and bends right, the Trail crosses over a further two roads. You will now be able to see the village of Biggin down the hill and to your left. About 400 yds after passing over the second road, take the footpath on the left towards the village, making for the white house you can see at the corner where the road bends away from the old railway – as you approach it you will notice that the path splits in two and the one you want bends slightly left, down a lane.

Coming to the corner of the road, turn left and almost immediately take the footpath on the left across two fields to the small group of houses ahead of you to the left.

Coming out on to the road turn left and, 100 yds later, take the footpath on the right down the head of Biggin Dale. This path was once proclaimed by a sign which read Public Footpath to Hartington but now, alas, only a stump of it remains. Perhaps this would be a good point to embark on a discussion of the vandalisation of footpath signs as a symptom of social degeneration in late 20th-century Britain. There again, perhaps not.

Follow the path down the dale and around to the left, pausing only to sigh a bit at the beauty of your surroundings and perhaps to fish out that packet of sandwiches you brought with you and munch them in contemplative, awestruck silence.

The dale bottom gets lower and lower and then joins the Dove valley from the left. Turn left and follow the river S down Mill Dale.

After a mile or so of this you come to some houses, an old mill and a road bridge. Turn left on to the road, away from the bridge and past the Derbyshire sign (though you never left the county) climbing uphill and bending slightly to the right.

Shortly the road straightens out and then starts to bend left, following the natural contours of the valley. Here take the footpath on the right, up a gully in the side of the hill. This is a very steep, long climb, so take your time.

At the top you'll pass through a gate-stile in a wall. Go straight over the small field you're in and turn left on the track on the other side, which will bring you to a place where four paths meet. According to the signposts, the path from Alsop to Dovedale runs right to left, and you are on the path from Milldale to Tissington. Isn't that reassuring?

Keep the wall on your left and you will soon come to another signpost. Take the footpath on the right here, up the hill and past Bostern Grange Farm to the left. Follow this path for about one mile until it starts to bend downhill to the left, crossing a minor road and coming out on to a second at a severe bend by a stone barn.

Turn right here for 300 yds, then take the footpath on the left leading SE downhill, across the brook at the bottom, and up the other side into a caravan park. Especially on the other side of the hill this path is well marked, and will bring you out on to a track on the side of the caravan park. Turn right, towards the bridge, but, just before you get to it, go left, dropping down on to the Tissington Trail, where another left turn will take you back to the car park half a mile later.

Bee Low from Oxlow Rake (Peak Forest)

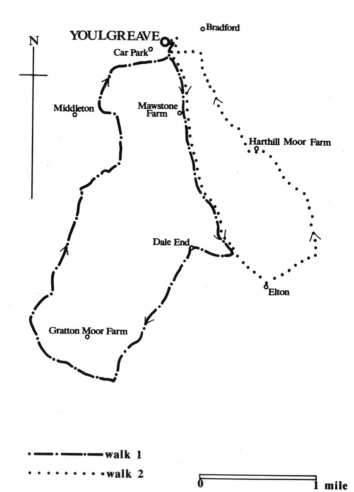

N

YOULGREAVE

Bradford

Car Park

Middleton

Mawstone Farm

Harthill Moor Farm

Dale End

Elton

Gratton Moor Farm

•—·—·—·— walk 1
· · · · · · · · walk 2

0   1 mile

YOULGREAVE

A pleasant village perched on the side of Bradford Dale, where the visitor has to make sure of parking the car in the car park or strict penalties will be invoked. The village does get a bit crowded with tourists, but once you are away from it and into the surrounding countryside – even the further away stretches of Bradford Dale below – the people thin out radically.

WALK 1: Youlgreave-Gratton Dale-Long Dale-Bradford Dale

A walk which takes you past relics of the Peak District's industrial past and through three very different sorts of dale, each with its own attractions.

Moderate going with climbing.
9 miles, 4 hrs.
Start SK205641.

Go into the village from the car park, and turn right downhill past the green corrugated-iron church hall and the toilets, coming to the river past the tea shop. Is it too early for a cuppa? Is it ever too early for a cuppa?

Cross the footbridge and go through the gate, uphill through a wood on the path which leads you up to Mawstone Farm. You're heading between the woods you can see at the top of the hill.

The path brings you out at Anthony Hill. You can remark at this point that you were at school with an Anthony Hill, and wonder whether it is the same one. Your companions will now think of you as a person with a wild and wacky sense of humour.

At the hill – Tony we used to call him, always had scabby knees and a cowlick – you pass under a cliff and an immense pile of boulders from the quarry workings. You can see indentations on many of the rocks where the lifting tackle was attached. You come out on to a road, where you should turn right for 200 yds then right again on the path to Gratton.

The end of this path at Dale End is practically impassable, being a quagmire which is home to countless venomous plants and insects. On the other side of the field, however, there is a farm track coming out on to the road a little further up.

When you are out on the road, turn left and make for the telephone box, to the right of which there is a path up Gratton Dale. This is a small but lovely dale – there is often a riot of birdsong and it is pleasantly wooded. The village of Gratton, by the way, which gave the dale its name, no longer exists, despite having been the centre of the largest parish in these parts in the Middle Ages. As you enter the dale, note the 18th-century limekiln to the right.

At the head of the dale (you can see a farm perched on the hilltop opposite you) turn right through two gates and into Long Dale, a broader, flatter, bleaker dale than Gratton.

After a mile the dale bends right with a wall running diagonally across the bottom. On the other side you should be able to see a path going diagonally up the hillside – take this and at the top go right through the gate, keeping the wall to your right.

After one mile the path meets a road where you carry on in the same direction (you have to do a little side-step left) and 600 yds later there are two footpath signs. Take the one on the right, and climb the hill, skirting the edge, coming down the other side to find a stile at the bottom left (NE) corner of the field. By following this path you'll come to a small, wooded dale which branches off to the left diagonally. Cross the stream in front of you and follow the path up the dale on the other side.

This path meanders, crossing the stream a few times, but keep to it and it will bring you to a big stone bridge which marks the head of Bradford Dale. From here it is a pleasant and easy walk back to Youlgreave, bringing you back to the footbridge and that tea shop.

WALK 2: Youlgreave-Elton-Robin Hood's Stride

An upland walk through limestone country that can be bleak or delightful, depending on the season and the weather. In any conditions, the weird rock formation known as Robin Hood's Stride is impressive.

Moderate going, some climbing.
6 miles, 3 hrs.
Start SK205641.

Follow the route for the previous walk as far as Anthony Hill, using the same joke if you think you can get away with it. Coming out on to the road turn right and then take footpath on the left up the hill to the village of Elton.

You come out near the church on a footpath signposted to Youlgreave. Turn right then left on the main road. After the church there is a footpath through the churchyard, and at the stile at the end of this head half right on a path which brings you out on to a minor road.

Turn left here and follow the road almost to its junction with the major road, bending severely to the right. Go straight on here, down a signposted footpath, keeping left of the trees, and this brings you to Robin Hood's Stride.

There is always a highly improbable folk-tale about places like this which says that the Devil was on his way to build himself a house but was frightened by a local hero (Robin Hood) so he dropped his stones and ran away. Either that or he chucked them at said hero but missed and they're still there to this day. In this case the story is completely true.

Oh alright then, however much those two pillars (they're called Weasel and Inaccessible) look like artefacts, it's a natural outcrop of gritstone which is less subject to erosion than the surrounding materials. The area is, however, stuffed with man-made features – downhill to the east you can see a cave in the woods where a hermit used to live, and it is worth taking the path down there to see the way he modified it to his own design.

Carry on along your original path on to the road and take the footpath directly opposite signposted to Youlgreave. When you emerge in the village, turn right on the road, cross the bridge and turn left immediately, following the river back to the footbridge and tea shop, where they do excellent cakes and bacon sandwiches, by the way.

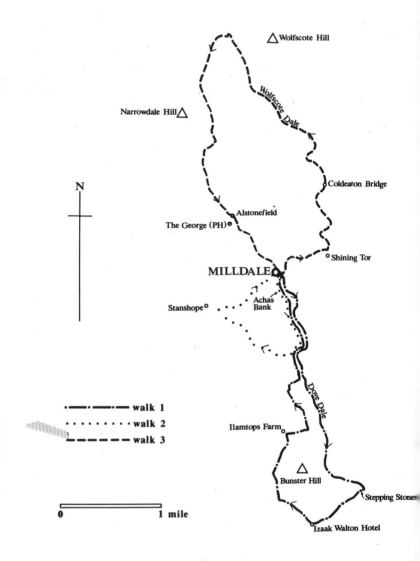

THE SOUTH-WEST

DOVEDALE

Dovedale is one of the most heavily touristy areas of the Peak District. The walker, in certain places and at certain times, has to share territory with picnickers, families, school parties, dogs and even fishermen. And yet, go a few yards off the beaten track and it is possible to find a combination of solitude and the spectacular scenery for which the dale is justly famous.

All three of the walks below start at the northern end of the dale, at the car park in Milldale. The real crowds tend to congregate at the southern end, near the huge car park, but, if you walk early enough in the morning, or late enough in the evening, or midweek at any time of the year other than high summer, even here the vast thronging hordes can be avoided.

WALK 1: Milldale-Bunster Hill

A walk along the whole length of the dale, returning through the delightful woods on the dale side.

Moderate and hard going, one climb.
7 miles, 3½ hrs.
Start SK138547.

Turn left out of the car park, into Milldale, past the tea and ices shop to your left. Is it too early to stop? On the other hand, can a refreshing brew be resisted? Tricky.

You've had your tea (wise decision) and the toilet block is to your right. Cross the stone bridge in front of you and take the main path up the left (east, for the technically minded) side of the dale. This takes you past Ilam Rock, Reynard's Cave and Tissington Spires, all of which should be admired or gazed at in awe, as appropriate.

Eventually, you come to the bottom of the dale. You were probably getting sick of all that natural beauty anyway. Cross the wall and the stepping stones over the river, and continue along the other side. Oh look, you're in Staffordshire.

A little further and there is a car park where a large man collects fees from people who did not have the foresight to park at Milldale.

Here turn right on the path signposted to Ilam. It goes past the Izaak Walton Hotel, named after the man who wrote *The Compleat Angler*, who was a big fish in these parts but couldn't spell complete. Or Isaac, come to that.

As you approach the hotel, do keep turning round to admire the view of the dale and Thorpe Cloud, the huge-seeming hill opposite.

Past the hotel there's a small paddock and a signpost to Ilam. You, however, are going up the hill (Bunster Hill) to your right, or at least to that dip you can see in its shoulder.

The shoulder makes a good sandwich-spot, and it is well worth making the small but strenuous detour to the top of Bunster Hill for the views.

Over the shoulder, follow the path round to the right to a wall, turning right here and climbing to the crossing point at the top left of the field. Head uphill and rightish, for the solitary tree to the right of a whole bunch of others, and two gates later you're in a green lane heading towards a farm.

At the end of the lane, turn right and head for the cottage you see perched on the hillside. The path goes almost up to the cottage, but veers off to the right at the last moment. Follow the path downhill and then left until you come to a rickety stile which takes you down into the wood. The going gets a bit rough here, especially if it has rained at any time in the past month, and the path is easy to lose, but try to keep heading north without losing too much height.

The wild flowers here in spring are amazing and if you come in summer the wood is teeming with brambles and strawberries. Eventually you will see the lone tower of Ilam Rock downhill and to your right. Pass down into the dale bottom, keeping to the right of the rock and trying not to slide into the almost inevitable rock climbers at the bottom. Turn left at the bottom.

Ignore the footbridge, staying on the left (west) side of the dale back to Milldale, going over Achas Bank where, again, the wild flowers grow with great profusion and variety.

WALK 2: Milldale-Hall Dale-Stanshope

An easy walk combining three completely different sorts of scenery – the spectacular Dovedale, the dry, wooded and narrow Hall Dale and limestone pasture on the top.

Moderate going, one gentle climb.
3 miles, 1½ hrs.
Start SK138547.

Take the signposted footpath out of Milldale past the toilets and up Achas Bank. Yes, it sounds as though the arbitration and conciliation people have gone into the money business, but it can be quite beautiful.

After one mile you come to a wall in front of you and a dry dale branching off to your right. Turn up this dale, almost back on yourself, and follow the bottom as it starts to climb out of the woods and on to the exposed limestone pastureland.

This brings you out on to a well-defined track leading into the hamlet of Stanshope. You could turn left and explore the place, if you like. It won't take much time. It's perhaps more sensible to turn right, uphill and through the gate, and you're then on the path which brings you back out in Milldale.

WALK 3: Milldale-Wolfscote Dale-Alstonefield

A beautiful riverside walk involving no great effort as it climbs very gently out of the dale bottom. This is the northern end of Dovedale, which is less popular because it is further from the car park. Perfect for a summer's evening, you can do this walk without seeing another soul apart, perhaps, from occasional fisherpersons, who don't really count.

Moderate going, gentle climbing.
6 miles, 2½ hrs.
Start SK138547.

Turn left out of the car park and left again along the road by the river. This road comes to a slanting T-junction. Turn right here, over the bridge into Derbyshire.

Just over the bridge, take the footpath on the left along the river bank signposted 'Beresford Dale, Wolfscote Dale and Hartington Leave no Litter'. Bully for them – neither do we.

There are a number of features of interest along the way, including an old water-powered pump which the farmers on the lip of the dale used to use to get their water from the river. Pass over one dry dale joining from the right, and eventually the dale forks, becoming Wolfscote Dale on the left, and Biggin Dale to the right.

Take the Wolfscote option, following it for three-quarters of a mile to its head where there is a stone-flagged footbridge on the left. Cross it then turn right, skirting the hill and trees to your left until you come to a wall. Cross this on to an overgrown path which brings you to open pastureland. You should now be facing SW and will soon find yourself in a green lane between fields. Keep heading SW until the track bends left and joins a track off right to Narrowdale Farm.

Go straight on, almost due S up the narrow defile in front of you. This is Narrowdale, so called because it's narrow. It's so deep and narrow, in fact, that it hardly gets any light (its north-south alignment helps, too) and the sun never shines here until at least one p.m., hence a local term 'Narrowdale noon', used to describe something which has been put off, postponed, delayed, deferred or procrastinated over. I'll tell you more about this later.

At the head of Narrowdale, bend right, joining a lane heading for a copse and some buildings. A hundred yards before the copse, take the path through the gate-stile on the left and, on reaching the road, turn left into Alstonefield.

In the village, turn left again and then down by the village green. Dilemma – is the George open? It usually is, and it's an excellent pub. Perhaps you'd like to pause and consider a pint or two?

Carry on past the church on your right and the amusing 'end of speed-limit' sign, and admire the gate into the churchyard with its sign forbidding the use of artificial flowers on graves, and 100 yds later take the footpath on the right which brings you back to Milldale.

Climbing to Hollins Cross from Castleton

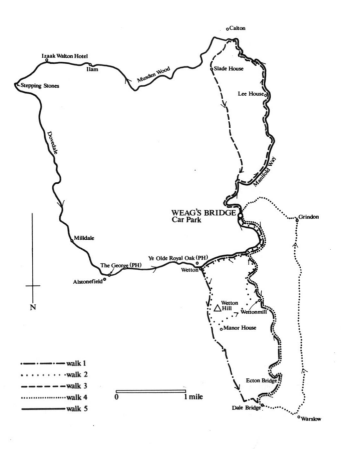

Calton
Izaak Walton Hotel
Ilam
Musden Wood
Slade House
Stepping Stones
Lee House
Dovedale
Manifold Way
WEAG'S BRIDGE
Car Park
Grindon
Milldale
Ye Olde Royal Oak (PH)
The George (PH)
Wetton
Alstonefield
Wetton Hill
Wettonmill
N
Manor House
Ecton Bridge
Dale Bridge
Warslow

——·——·—— walk 1
············· walk 2
—— —— —— walk 3
················· walk 4
————————— walk 5

0   1 mile

MANIFOLD VALLEY

The Manifold Valley is the next one along from Dovedale and is, to my mind, just as spectacular. It is less popular with tourists, perhaps because it is a bit more difficult to get to. Getting to the starting point of these walks, the car park at Weag's Bridge, involves a very hairy drive whether you approach it from the west via Grindon or from Alstonefield in the east, but once there some of the walking through the spectacular scenery of the valley is very easy, thanks to a group of businessmen at the turn of the century who built a light railway along the valley bottom to take passengers and minerals from Hulme End to Leek, less than ten miles by road, almost 20 by rail. The railway lasted less than 30 years, and is now a footpath. Seemed like a good idea at the time, though.

WALK 1: Weag's Bridge-Wetton-Ecton

A magnificent walk which combines the glories of the Manifold Valley with the spectacular scenery up on Wetton Hill and Ecton Hill from where, on a clear day, you can see for miles.

Easy going, one long hard climb and one steep descent.
9 miles, 4 hrs.
Start SK100542.

Take the Manifold track N out of the car park. After three-quarters of a mile you pass a spectacular cave on the hill top to your right – Thor's Cave. Just as the valley bends left here, take the footpath off to the right which crosses a concrete and steel footbridge over the river bed.

On the other side branch slightly left through a gate stile and climb uphill through the wood. Some way uphill you will come to a path climbing off to the right which goes to Thor's Cave, and it is well worth making the trip as the cave is very impressive, especially on a summer's evening when the sun is in the west and lights the whole thing up.

Once out of the wood there is still a bit of a climb until you reach Wetton, but there are magnificent views of the valley behind you.

Coming to Wetton, carry straight on into the village along the road until it bends sharply downhill to the right, at which point an interesting dilemma presents itself. The path we want goes up the little lane which leads off to the left from this corner, but Ye Olde Royal Oak is 200 yds to the right. One ingenious solution to this dilemma, I have found, is to go down the hill to the Royal Oak, have a pint or two and then turn around and come back. Simple, but effective.

At the corner, take the lane leading diagonally away from the village, and along this there is a footpath signposted to Back of Ecton which you should follow, climbing Wetton Hill. On the other side of the hill, keep heading for Back of Ecton, which you can now see on the hill ahead of you and to the left.

Emerging on a bending minor road, turn left.* Two hundred yards up the hill there is a gate on the right, which you should go through, keeping the drystone wall at the top to your right. Over the brow of the hill, half a mile later, there is a broad, sloping pasture with a square barn at the other side perched on top of what looks like a tower. At the wall before it, turn left downhill, bringing yourself out in Ecton.

You come into a courtyard with an arched entrance. Turn right down on to the road, then left, then, 200 yds later, turn right opposite a cottage on to a track along the valley bottom, the one to the left, bringing you to the tunnel through which the valley road emerges. Here, turn left past the entrance to Swainsley Hall and over Ecton Bridge. Shortly after this, take the gated road with the No Buses sign on the right.

After more than a mile you come to Dale Farm. Turn right over the bridge unless (a) you fancy a cuppa in the cafe at Wettonmill and (b) it is open. On the other side of the bridge turn left and take either of the two roads you can see as they join up again 500 yds later. Where the roads rejoin, there is a gated footbridge crossing the river. Cross this and you are now back on the Manifold track which will bring you back to the car park.

*You can cut the walk short here by carrying on to the left along this road, uphill, and then turning left along the footpath past the dramatic Sugarloaf, which brings you back to Wettonmill.

WALK 2: Weag's Bridge-Wetton-Wetton Hill

A shorter version of the previous walk which still allows you to get a good impression of the Manifold Valley and adds a dramatic descent back to the Manifold at the back of Wetton Hill.

Mainly easy going with one long climb and descent.
5 miles, 2½ hrs.
Start SK100542.

This is perhaps the option to choose if you fancy a walk with a pub in the middle of it, or if you spend too much time in Wetton, or if you simply fancy a dramatic walk and there isn't much time. Follow the previous walk through Wetton, and, if desired, into the Old Royal Oak, and up Wetton Hill.

Just over the brow of Wetton Hill the paths diverge. Follow the wall around to the left, going past the gate with barbed wire on it, and round to the bottom of the small valley which emerges ahead of you and to the left.

Cross the footbridge, and turn left, following this valley as it falls down to meet the Manifold. You are nearly there when it bends sharply left and enters some woods. Where it meets the road, turn right and almost immediately left across the gated footbridge which brings you on to the Manifold track and back to the car park.

WALK 3: Weag's Bridge-Carlton-Cart Low-Soles Hollow

A pleasant walk along the eastern loop of the Hamps, immediately south of the Manifold, through a gentle, wooded dale, over limestone hills and down through a beautiful natural gully.

Easy going with one steep climb and one tricky descent.
6 miles, 2½ hrs.
Start SK100542.

Go S out of the car park, across the road. To the right of the bridge, take the path over the stile running to the right of and parallel to the lane to Beeston Tor Farm. Continue on this path for a quarter of a mile, until the valley branches right and left under Beeston Tor.

The route follows the valley to the right, but you might like to consider making for the cliffs of Beeston Tor, if they are not stuffed with rock climbers, to see St Bertram's Cave which is associated with both St Bertram (obviously – that's why it's called St Bertram's Cave) and Prehistoric Man, or Prehistoric Person, as she is now known.

Follow the meandering course of the Hamps upstream (and uphill), heading more or less SSW, eventually passing Lea House Farm, where they do teas and sandwiches, on your left.*

After another half a mile, and one more crossing of the Hamps, take the waymarked footpath uphill to the left. This means a bit of a climb, but it is not too bad. At the top there is what would be a spectacular view, were it not for the quarry workings at Cauldon to the SW, which mar the vista spectacularly.

Follow the footpath as it winds along the top to a green lane, at which point turn right on the path to Calton. In the village, turn left on the back road, past a cottage with the slopingest roof you'll ever see, taking the second footpath on the left, after a converted barn to your right.

*You can cut the walk short here by crossing the rickety wooden footbridge and climbing the small dale opposite to join the route up on Cart Low.

This brings you to a minor road, and there's a footpath directly opposite climbing gently uphill to an attractive stone-built farmhouse (Slade House). In the farmyard, turn left up a semi-metalled cart track which takes you uphill on to Cart Low.

This brings you to a minor road with a house to your right and a farm in front of you and to the left. Head along the path opposite, down the bottom of the valley which is just starting. Keeping as low as you can, eventually you will find yourself in a deep depression (ha bloody ha) heading for a gate into some woods.

The going through this wooded gully, Soles Hollow, can be a bit tricky, especially after rain, but it is extremely attractive. At the bottom you emerge, hey presto, back into the Hamps valley. Turn right, and follow it back to the car park.

WALK 4: Weag's Bridge-Ecton-Warslow-Grindon

A walk up the Manifold and on to the beautiful surrounding Staffordshire hills with views down into the valley.

Easy-moderate going with three climbs.
9 miles, 3½ hrs.
Start SK100542.

Follow the Manifold track N out of the car park and wind with it past Thor's Cave until you join the road. Turn left after the footbridge and follow the road N, crossing the bridge towards Wettonmill, where there are toilets and a cafe.

Just at the entrance to Wettonmill, bend left with the track, then sharply right then left again on the other side of the small paddock to your left. You should now be on a gated track running parallel to the river, and about 50 feet above it. Follow this north for just over a mile as it winds through woodlands and down to the riverbank, noting, as you approach Ecton Bridge, the working stone-built round dovecote on the other side of the river.

At Ecton Bridge the track joins a minor road. Turn left over the bridge and then right opposite the road tunnel, following the path to Ecton proper.

At the end of this track, make your way up on to the road and follow it to the left. On reaching a junction, turn left on the road to Warslow.

Over the bridge the road starts to climb and bend to the right. Take the waymarked footpath on the left to Warslow, bending slightly right after the first large field.

In Warslow, turn left and, just before the school, left again down the lane signposted as a dead end. At the end of this is Villa Farm, and the footpath runs through the farmyard to the left.

The footpath is well waymarked and really presents few problems as it heads due S to Grindon. It crosses two minor roads and, as it climbs towards Grindon, one farm lane, but the continuations are directly opposite.

Emerging into Grindon with the church to your right, you will come to a road where you should turn left then quickly right on to the back road. A little way along this road on your left is a white house called The White House and on the other side of this on the left is the footpath back down to the Manifold Valley, though the signpost saying so fell down years ago.

At the back of the houses, bend sharp left along the lane, taking the footpath diagonally right downhill 200 yds later. This footpath more or less follows the bottom of the valley you are in. Soon you will be able to see a small barn – keep well to the left of it and, when you reach the wall it is on the other side of, strike uphill to the left, which brings you to the road.

Turn right and, as the road bends crazily to the left, take the footpath to the left of the barn by the side of the road, going straight downhill and cutting out the loop in the road. This brings you out on to the road again with Weag's Bridge to the right and the car park just to the left of it.

WALK 5: Weag's Bridge-Calton-Ilam-Dovedale-Milldale-Alstonefield-Wetton

The sheer distance involved and the amount of climbing make this a walk only for the very fit. Having said that, the rewards are enormous – the Dove and Manifold Valleys can be compared and contrasted, the woodland explored and the hills delighted in.

Moderate, occasionally hard going, 2 big climbs.
15 miles, 7 hrs.
Start SK100542.

Head S out of the car park, over the road and along the track to the right of Weag's Bridge along the right bank of the river to Beeston Tor, at which point fork right along the Hamps for two miles.

Pass Lea House Farm on your left, and half a mile later take the footpath to the left uphill. It zigzags a bit, but eventually comes to a green lane leading off to the right to Calton.

Coming to the village, turn left on the road and follow it for about 500 yds, past a junction to your left, until it starts to bend right. Here, take the track on the left, leading down into the head of a small valley.

Where the track turns off right, carry straight on downhill into Musden Wood, keeping to the valley bottom for well over a mile. This is beautiful at most times of the year, particularly, perhaps, in the autumn when the leaves are turning.

At the end of the wood, there's a track leading 100 yds to the road, which you should take, turning right immediately on the footpath heading SE over the brow of the hill and down, across the river into Ilam.

Turn right on the road then, once past the entrance to the Youth Hostel (left), take the footpath on the left signposted to Dovedale. This goes past the Izaak Walton Hotel and comes into Dovedale opposite the car park. Turn left and follow the road to the stepping stones, cross over and continue up the dale on the other side, coming eventually to the tiny hamlet of Milldale.

Crossing the stone bridge, ahead of you and to the left there is a narrow lane, marked as a dead end, with a little tea shop on the left-hand side. Go down here, past the tea shop, no past it don't stop to buy . . . oh alright then.

Immediately after the shop take the footpath on the left uphill to Alstonefield. It brings you out on a lane leading left into Alstonefield (in fact it's the lane you just left in Milldale, and it's marked as a dead end here too. Funny, that).

Once past the church and at the village green, take the left fork past the George. Hang on a moment, 'past the George'. There is something deeply unsettling about that phrase – why not drop in for a pint?

Continuing on to the main road and past the sign boasting of the village's status as the most well kept in Staffordshire, you come to a T-junction, with a footpath opposite to the right, by the old school. Take the footpath, leading more or less due W, then bending off left before continuing the same line.

The path crosses two metalled roads in uncomplicated fashion before emerging on to a third. Turn right here and, taking the left fork, follow the road into Wetton.

Coming into the village, turn right up the main street, past Ye Olde Royal Oak. Hang on a moment, 'past Ye Olde Royal Oak' . . . (see 'George' above). Turn left at the top of the hill, and follow the road to where it forks, taking the path downhill at the fork which keeps close to the right-hand road.

At the wrong time of year, this is one of the muddiest places in the universe, but bear with it as it will soon get worse. Admiring the splendid views down into the Manifold Valley, follow the bottom of the shallow gully you are now in into the woods, where it can get very slippery indeed.

At the bottom, cross the footbridge over the riverbed and turn left on to the Manifold track. This takes you back to the car park.

N

Lower Fleetgreen

Little
Fernyford

Spout
Farm

Herbage

Revidge

Upper Elkstone

Old Mixon Hay

Breech
Ryecroft

Brownlow

Waterhouse

BUTTERTON

Butterton
Moor
End

Coxon
Green

Onecote Jervis Arms (PH)

Wetton

Sheldon Farm

Ford

Grindon

Weag
Bridge

Felthouse

•—·—·—·—·— walk 1
· · · · · · · · · walk 2
– – – – – – walk 3
················· walk 4

0   1 mile

BUTTERTON

A charming little village (with a nice pub) amid rolling hills. Approaching the village by car from the south (from Grindon) is a laugh, and much to be recommended – there's a ford, and it's not immediately obvious how to get out of it. Parking is a bit of a problem, though there's a substantial bit of verge and lay-by north of the church.

WALK 1: Butterton-Shawfield-Upper Elkstone

A tremendous variety of landscapes – the rolling hills near Butterton, low-lying moorland to the north, and then the more angular, craggy hills around the Elkstones – make for an interesting walk.

Moderate going, several climbs and descents.
9 miles, 4 hrs.
Start SK075566.

Leave Butterton on the signposted footpath north of the church, and follow it due N to the Warslow road. Opposite and to the right is the Elkstones road, and the footpath you want is just off it to the right. Proceed due north, uphill, along a distinct path which eventually becomes a narrow lane. When 800 yds later the lane bends NE, carry straight on to another road.

The next path is opposite and to the left (and signposted). This brings you out on to more open, scrubby moorland. Over the crest of this hill, still going northish, you descend, to the right of a farm, on to yet another road. Turn right here along the road for 250 yds, taking the next lane on the left. This almost immediately bifurcates. Fork right, downhill, along a very squishy (if it has rained at any time in the last year) track. Squelch your way to the brook, cross the bridge, and take the footpath on the left parallel to the brook.

This will soon start to climb slightly and bring you to the right of a farm and on to a lane. Follow this to the right until it, too, bifurcates (there's a lot of it about). Go left up to the road.

Cross the stile opposite and to your left and cross a couple of fields to yet another road (the path simply cuts out the corner). The next path (signposted) is opposite and to your left. It descends, prettily, SW to meet that same brook you squelched across about two miles back, and then bends due S to climb that steep hill in front of you.

You come, after a bit of a slog, to another road, which you need to cross, taking the footpath opposite to the right of a barn. Upper Elkstone is due S of here, on the other side of some lovely, but a bit up-and-downy, countryside. When you have gone down for quite a way, and then have had to go back up the other side, you will appreciate why Upper Elkstone is called Upper Elkstone. It's because it's higher up than Lower Elkstone, and it's full of elks.

You come up a narrow lane and turn left on to the impossibly winding main street of the village. (The bit about the elks was a lie.) Take the dead-end road on the right, by the side of the church, which soon bends left and becomes a footpath leading SE along the side of the hill. It brings you, after a mile or so without a major change of direction, to the main road. There's a footpath opposite, which will take you over a few fields to a minor road, where it is a simple matter of turning right to get back to Butterton.

WALK 2: Butterton-Shawfield-Upper Elkstone-Onecote-Grindon Moor

An extended version of Walk 1, this walk takes you over even more varied scenery, including Grindon Moor.

Moderate going, some climbing.
11 miles, 5 hrs.
Start SK075566.

Follow Walk 1 as far as Upper Elkstone, turning right on to the village's main street, then taking the signposted footpath on the left. It follows a windy little lane which bends around to the left and then heads due S, climbing slightly for more than half a mile.

You come to a road at a farm called Breech. Cross the road and take the footpath opposite, following a drainage ditch S into some more rather soggy ground. This is the time to reflect on what a good idea it might have been to put dubbin or wax on your boots this morning.

In a little under a mile you will be up on Butterton Moor, looking down on the village of Onecote. Descend, and make your way to the main road, following a lane to the left when you reach a small group of buildings near the bottom of the hill. Turn right when you get to the road.

The Jervis Arms is 300 yds further on, you might be interested to know, and it does a good pint (and good food, if it's that time). The path, however, turns left after less than 100 yds, up the narrow lane to Home Farm, which doubles back on the road. Past the farm itself, carry straight on when the lane bends right, which will take you across Grindon Moor which has, if you're interested, some unusual mosses growing on it.

The footpath back to Butterton is directly opposite when you get to the road.

WALK 3: Butterton-Oncote-Mixon Hill

This is a walk through the hilly country around the road known as Morridge (moor-edge, so called because it's the edge of the moors), so as well as the pleasures of the countryside itself, the views to the west can be quite spectacular.

Moderate going with some climbing, none of it too hard.
8½ miles, 4 hrs.
Start SK075566.

Take the south road out of the village, past the tea-room, taking the footpath on the right just after the two-angled bends. This follows the right bank of a small brook and leads almost due W to a farm building half a mile from the village. Here the path becomes more distinct, and soon bends slightly S to meet the Grindon road. Cross over, on to Grindon Moor (a National Trust property, so it is festooned with signs) now heading WSW on to a farm lane which will bring you down on to the main road near Onecote.

Turn left on the road and walk on into the village, turning right past the Jervis Arms (it's far too early to go in). You will soon notice the very grand-looking Onecote Grange on your right. Here take the footpath on the right signposted to the Mermaid (it's a pub but, alas and alack, you are not going that far – perhaps you should have nipped into the Jervis but it's too late now).

This takes you over a footbridge and then a little way up the hill opposite. At the first wall you come to, turn left, following the stream as it winds its way around to the north in what becomes a rather attractive little valley.

After nigh on two miles of this, you come to a farm called Old Mixon Hay. It is close to the Morridge road and there is a small wood to your left. Here take the lane on the right, going due E uphill. Climb over the hill, cross the young River Hamps on the other side and keep following the path due E over another hill until you come to a road. (A point of local natural interest: this is an isolated bit of road and, in the mating season, by emerging stealthily, you can sometimes catch unawares pairs of the Randy Staffordshire Office Worker in their tell-tale striped shirtage and Ford Fiesta, going through their courtship ritual on the large verges). Cut the corner by taking the footpath opposite and you will emerge at a farmhouse called Breech.

Turn left on to the road, taking the next footpath on the left which will take you NE to a farm called Ryecroft. It is not always easy to find this path so you could always take the lane a little further on – the path joins it later – but don't tell anyone I told you to.

When you get to the next farm, take the footpath on the right, leading SE along the side of the hill, and bringing you back to the main Warslow road after almost a mile. Cross the road and take the footpath opposite, and when you come to a minor road after crossing four fields, turn right to return to Butterton.

WALK 4: Butterton-Manifold Valley-Grindon-Ford

A walk through some charming and varied countryside – moor, the steep-sided Manifold Valley, and the low-lying, wooded Hamps – and a couple of beautiful villages – Grindon and Ford.

Moderate going but treacherous in wet weather, steep climbs.
9 miles, 4 hrs.
Start SK075566.

Take the Grindon road from Butterton church, heading S downhill, until you come to the ford. Here, turn left by the side of the Hoo Brook. You are now on a footpath which follows the brook as it tumbles down some 400 feet into the Manifold Valley. This is all pretty much plain sailing, navigation-wise, but do take care if it has been raining as this bit of the walk can be slippery and nasty.

You will walk SE for about three-quarters of a mile until you reach a wood, then turn NE, following the perimeter of the wood, descending for another half a mile on to the floor of the Manifold Valley.

You will find yourself on a minor road. Turn right and follow it SSE for 500 yds, until it bends left and crosses the course of the River Manifold. Here, take the gated footpath on the right and follow the course of the former Manifold Valley Light Railway for a mile, until you come to a car park.

At the road at the other end of the car park, take the footpath opposite and slightly to the right, climbing SW steeply uphill to meet the same road as it bends back on itself. Turn left and follow the bend round to the right, taking the footpath on the left 75 yds later which drops down after one field to the bottom of a small valley. Here turn right and climb to the head of the valley in Grindon.

You will emerge by the side of a cottage called the White House. Turn left on the road, past the phone box and school and make for the Cavalier (a pub, not a 17th-century royalist or automobile manufactured by Vauxhall).

Turn right on the road here, and take the footpath on the left by the side of the pub. This starts off heading WSW, but gradually bends SW to bring you out on to a minor road in the middle of nowhere about a mile later.

Coming on to the road, turn left and then take the footpath on the right opposite a big red barn. This bends NW, downhill at an angle, and follows the River Hamps to the tiny hamlet of Ford.

You emerge through a lightly wooded stretch on to a bend in the road. Turn left and, before the road has completed the bend, take the footpath on the right past a small farmhouse. (The footpath isn't signposted as such, but there are circles on the gateposts in a relic from some 1970s waymarking scheme.)

Follow this footpath (more or less constantly NNE) uphill and over Grindon Moor to the Grindon Road. Once you have crossed this, the footpath directly opposite takes you back down into Butterton.

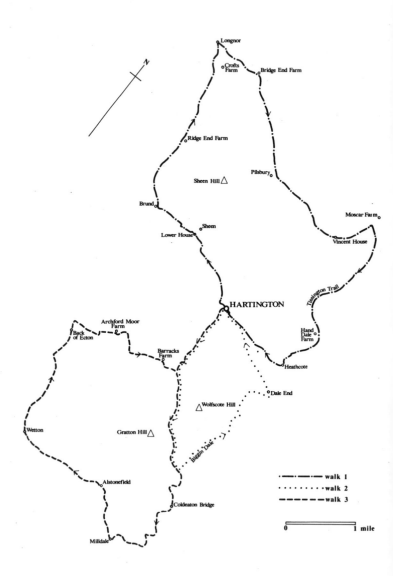

Longnor

Crofts Farm

Bridge End Farm

Ridge End Farm

Pilsbury

Sheen Hill △

Moscar Farm

Brund

Sheen

Lower House

Vincent House

Tissington Trail

HARTINGTON

Archford Moor Farm

Back of Ecton

Hand Dale Farm

Barracks Farm

Heathcote

Dale End

Wolfscote Hill △

Wetton

Gratton Hill △

Biggin Dale

Alstonefield

Coldeaton Bridge

Milldale

—·—·— walk 1
············ walk 2
— — — walk 3

0   1 mile

HARTINGTON

Hartington can get a bit crowded, especially at the weekends in summer, so it does have its drawbacks. On the other hand, it has plenty of advantages – it's immensely pretty, it's close to Dovedale and the Manifold Valley, and it has a brilliant cheese shop, the outlet of the factory where most Stilton cheese is made. A baby Stilton is quite a purchase and lasts for ages, but don't take it walking with you as both you and it will end up walking home alone.

WALK 1: Hartington-Sheen-Longnor-Pilsbury-Parsley Hay-Heathcote

Gentle rolling pasture, riverside farmland and high limestone pasture – a fine, easy, long walk through changing scenery with splendid panoramas of the surrounding hills.

Moderate going, one serious climb.
13 miles, 6 hrs.
Start SK128604.

You're standing in the market place with your back to the Devonshire and the Charles Cotton to your left. Walk forward. Turn left and, just left of the cheese shop, take the lane leading to the cheese factory. Follow it a while.

Just before you get to the factory, take the footpath on the right, leading past a farm and then downhill over a stream – the Dove. This leads you over the steep but low hill into Sheen. Coming down into the village, make for that Tudor pile you can see to your right, coming out on to the road just to the left of it.

On the road turn left and almost immediately take the footpath on the right to Brund, which heads more or less due W and soon joins a lane down into that thriving metropolis.

Turn right on to the road and then, where it bends right a couple of hundred yards later, take the footpath on the left signposted to Longnor. This meanders alongside the Manifold for almost three miles before bringing you out in Longnor, and very pleasant it is too.

You come into the village through a farmyard, turning right on to a lane which brings you out on to the main road. Turn right again and follow the road out of the village, taking the left fork towards Crowdecote, downhill, where it splits.

At the very bottom of the hill take the signposted footpath on the right which immediately bends left and crosses a footbridge over the Dove. On the other side you could turn left and nip into the Packhorse in Crowdecote, but the walk turns right down the lane and continues SE alongside the Dove until it starts climbing by the earthworks at Pilsbury Castle some one-and-a-half miles later.

This is a bit of a climb, but the views as you ascend broaden out in the most spectacular fashion, making it a very rewarding one. You soon find yourself on upland pasture by the hamlet of Pilsbury.

Cross a road and continue up a broad, shallow valley. At the next wall there's a signpost saying footpath to Hartington off to the right. Ignore it*, and carry straight on, bending left when a road heaves into view ahead of you to your right half a mile later.

This takes you downhill, across a road and through a farmyard. Go right and then quickly left at the other end of the yard, past a small quarry and uphill. Another dip and a climb through another farmyard will bring you on to the disused railway that is now the High Peak Trail. Turn right and follow it S.

You will soon pass a car park, picnic site and cycle hire centre on your left. You can sometimes get refreshments here too. A little way after that, the railway forks; one branch (the Cromford and High Peak Railway) going off left towards Matlock, the other, the one you are following, heading more directly S to Ashbourne via Hartington.

Stay on this trail until you come to the old Hartington Station. Go past the car park and the old signal box. There is a nature trail signboard to your left and the footpath to Hartington goes off to the right, though, in fact, it only goes as far as Heathcote.

You come out into this tiny village having turned left on to a lane. Cross the road and follow the lane opposite, taking the footpath on the right 200 yds later, before a large collection of farm buildings to your left. This footpath crosses one field and then swings downhill SW, keeping just right of the wall.

You come to a road. Take the lane opposite and then turn right at the first opportunity. This brings you to the back road into Hartington. Turn left downhill and you're practically there.

*Unless you want to shorten the walk, leaving yourself only two miles back to Hartington instead of the five remaining on the full route, in which case turn right, following the path S uphill. It's actually quite a pleasant walk, following the upper slope of the upper Dove valley to a minor road, where a simple right turn will bring you back to Hartington.

WALK 2: Hartington-Beresford Dale-Biggin Dale

A short but delightful walk exploring two dales near Hartington and climbing gently up on to the limestone plateau before returning.

Easy-moderate going with a big, gentle climb.
5½ miles, 2½ hrs.
Start SK128604.

Take the Warslow road from the market place, past the Charles Cotton, to the pottery on the left. Pause to browse amongst the traditional Derbyshire terracotta including traditional Derbyshire strawberry planters and traditional Derbyshire things for growing hanging plants in, and take the footpath signposted to Beresford Dale to the right. There are a number of footpaths diverging at this point, so you can get confused, but it's easy as long as you keep right and head due S.

This path undulates a little, but soon descends into the beautiful, wooded Beresford Dale. This area is very popular with anglers. Do not attempt to engage any of them in conversation as they are anti-social. Otherwise they wouldn't be anglers, would they?

The woods stop and the countryside opens out to your right. Bend slightly left, staying on the same side of the river, and you enter another dale – Wolfscote Dale. Not so many trees, but deeper and steeper. Probably still some anglers, too.

After a mile, another dale joins from the left. Turn left and go up it, keeping the wall to your right. The ground here can be a little tricky, especially in the wet, so be careful. At least there are no more anglers.

You start climbing now, very gently, for another mile, until this dale (Biggin Dale) forks. Take the path off to the left, keeping the wall to your right.

This small dale climbs, bending round to the right, and eventually broadens out. By now you should be on the beginnings of a lane or track, taking you past the sewage works.

When the lane meets a road and ends, turn left for 100 yds, then again down a very narrow lane between a small group of farm buildings. This climbs gently uphill for 600 yds, and over the crest of the hill you will be able to see your way down into Hartington – keep on the lane until it ends at a road, then turn left down the hill.

WALK 3: Hartington-Dovedale-Wetton-Archford Moor-Beresford Dale

A long walk through some of the southern Peak's most spectacular scenery and villages.

Moderate and easy going, two big climbs.
13½ miles, 5½ hrs.
Start SK128604.

Follow Walk 2 into Beresford Dale and Wolfscote Dale, carrying straight on past the entrance to Biggin Dale. Follow the path down the left side of the River Dove for another mile-and-a-half, until you come to a road.

Turn right, over the bridge, and left down the road to Milldale. Once in the hamlet, turn right, and then right again almost immediately, past the small tea-and-ices shop.

Just past this, take the footpath on the left, steeply uphill, which brings you out on a lane near Alstonefield church. Turn left and follow the lane into the village, past the George (one of the best pubs in the Peak), on the left side of the green.

Coming out on to the main road, turn left once more and make for the T-junction. Take the lane opposite and right which gives on to a footpath heading downhill and SW, before turning W at the stile over the next wall.

Follow this over fields (and a couple of narrow minor roads) for a mile, until you come out on to a third road bounded by dry-stone walls. Turn right and, 200 yds later, fork left. Forking left once more, 300 yds further on, will bring you to the crossroads at the bottom of Wetton. Turn right and climb up the village street, past Ye Olde Royal Oak (heading NNW).

After 300 yds you come to a corner – the road bends left, but there is a lane off diagonally in front of you. Take this, and then the footpath uphill signposted to Back of Ecton. This takes you over Wetton Hill, and it is a truly glorious climb. On the other side, where the paths fork, keep right, heading gradually downhill, towards some houses on the hill opposite, on the well-defined path.

The path then bends left and climbs a bank to meet a lane at Back of Ecton. Turn right, coming to another lane after 150 yds. Carry straight on here, along the side of the hill, for half a mile, past some houses, until the road bends right and goes sharply downhill.

Where it bends left again 150 yds later, take the footpath which carries straight on. This climbs again to meet another road after 500 yds. Turn left and take the footpath on the right after 100 yds, downhill towards a farm. At the wall of the farmyard, bend around to the right and continue on your former heading once past it. This takes you across a couple more fields to yet another road.

Turn right here and head SE, over a crossroads and bend around to the left, heading ENE after another 300 yds. Follow this road for another three-quarters of a mile until it brings you to Beresford Dale, where it is simply a case of turning left on the riverside footpath and retracing your steps to Hartington.

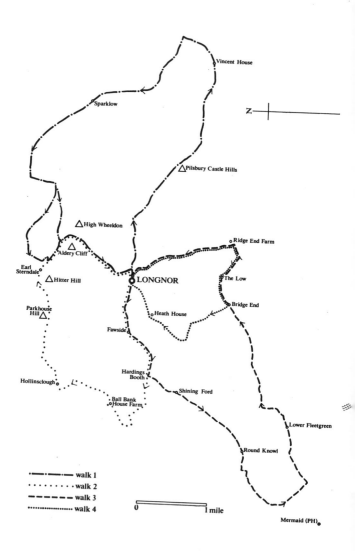

LONGNOR

Once a thriving market town, Longnor is now one of those places caught in a kind of limbo between the old and the new. It retains much of its character (and many of its old characters – ancient rustics who, on a summer's day, can be seen sitting in the market place doing nowt) and has not really geared up to the tourist trade in a big way (yet). On the other hand, the market has long been a thing of the past – the market place is now a car park – and the place is now stuffed with artists and craftspersons who do, it must be said, contribute to an air of bustle in a village which could so easily have been left to wither and decay.

The hills around here are wonderful and various: there is limestone moor to the east and south-east; to the south lie the Dove and Manifold valleys; to the west is the eastern edge of the Western Moors, and to the north are some dramatic, craggy peaks which are reminiscent in shape, if not in scale, of the West Highlands.

WALK 1: Longnor-Pilsbury-Parsley Hay-Earl Sterndale

A superb walk climbing up on to the limestone plateau, turning north and making a spectacular descent into Earl Sterndale and Longnor.

Moderate going with one long climb.
10 miles, 4 hrs.
Start SK088649.

From the market place, facing the old market hall (now a crafts centre), turn right past the chip shop and the Cheshire Cheese, leaving the village following the signs to Crowdecote. Where the road forks, 400 yds out of the village, take the left, downhill.

At the very bottom of the hill, just before a left bend, take the footpath on the right, bringing you to a footbridge over the Dove. Cross this (into Derbyshire) following the footpath on the right on the other side, signposted to Pilsbury. It is, after all, far too early to make the detour to the left and drop in at the Packhorse in Crowdecote, for all that it is a nice pub. You've got some serious walking to do.

After a mile the path starts to climb to the left of a curious outcrop known as Pilsbury Castle Hills, so called because it is close to Pilsbury and has a castle, well, an earthwork construction, on it. As you climb, the views behind you become ever more exciting, particularly those of the hills to the north of Longnor, amongst which you will be walking later.

71

This brings you out on to a minor road by the hamlet of Pilsbury. Take the footpath opposite signposted to Hartington and Parsley Hay, going up a broad, shallow valley. At the end of the first big field the footpath to Hartington goes off to the right, but carry straight on, following the path as it bends left and descending to meet a minor road.

The path goes through the farmyard on the other side, bending quickly right and left and climbing up past a small quarry working. Over the crest of this hill you can see the old railway, now the High Peak Trail, running along the hillside opposite below the busy A515. Just below the trail is a farm on a minor road.

The path comes out on to the minor road and continues up a grassy bank and through a gate into the farmyard which is slightly to the right. From here it is less than 200 yds to the trail, where you should turn left.

Follow the trail northwards until it stops – about three miles. This is pleasant and easy walking, and there are good views, especially to your left, of the countryside. The verges here are also good places for wild flowers.

At the end of the trail there's a sort of a T-junction with a track. Take this to the left, following the sign to Earl Sterndale, for 400 yds, until you come to a footpath on the right, which goes, not over a stile, but over a sort of lowering of the wall.

Here bend half left, keeping well away from the quarry workings, and head ESE, making for a point about 100 yds down from the right-hand corner of the field. This is the path which brings you downhill on to the top road into Sterndale.

It is possible, here, to turn right into the village. The chief advantage of this is that it takes you very close to the Quiet Woman – a good pub, with a deeply misogynistic sign showing the headless body of a woman. The story is that a local woman, 'Chattering Chateris', tormented her husband and the other villagers so much that he cut her head off and they named the pub after her and paid for her headstone. Earl Sterndale has still to see a New Man take up residence. To rejoin the route, turn right out of the pub and follow the Crowdecote road.

Coming on to the road from the hill, take the footpath opposite which brings you on to a steep farm track. Follow this downhill, turning left on to the Crowdecote road at the bottom. This road bends round to the right between Aldery Cliff and High Wheeldon. Where it bends left again, just before a barn on the left side of the road, turn right down a lane to the left of a house. Where this lane bends right towards a farm a few hundred yards later, cross the stile in front of you and carry on in the same direction, crossing a bridge then climbing back up into Longnor.

Depending on where you left the car, it's useful to note on the very last leg that the main path you can see climbing the bank into Longnor brings you out at the very eastern edge of the village. Halfway up this path, there is a path off to the right which takes you more directly uphill and on to the back streets, from where getting to the market place is easy-peasy.

WALK 2: Longnor-Hollinsclough

A walk over moors and then through the marvellous craggy peaks to the north of Longnor and Hollinsclough.

Moderate (sometimes boggy) going, with climbs.
8 miles, 3½ hrs.
Start SK088649.

Head W out of market place, over the main Warslow and Ashbourne road and past the Horseshoe. Where the road bends left take the footpath carrying straight on, dipping then climbing, almost parallel to the Hollinsclough road on your right, until you come to a farm.

Take the path around this to the left, and then follow it downhill and up the opposite side of the valley to a road. Turn right on to the road.

Half a mile along this road, you will be able to see a garage uphill from you. Take the track on the right opposite a road joining from the left.

You have to do a bit of detouring here because of the way the footpaths lie: just after some farm buildings you have to turn left on to another lane for 200 yds, then turn right on to a footpath downhill opposite yet another lane joining from the left. On the hill opposite you can see a farm to the right. It is this you are making for.

After 200 yds of steep descent, you come to a stile. Cross it and bear right, making for the protruding corner of wall you can see on the right. When you get here head as directly for the farm opposite as you can. At the bottom of the hill there's a footbridge over the brook, and on the other side crossing a stile in the top right corner of the paddock you are in will put you into a lane, which in turn will bring you to the farmyard.

Keep left of the farmyard, doubling back to the right once you are past it. Crossing three more stiles and climbing about 200 feet will bring you to the corner of a road. Make your way on to the main road, and turn right then quickly left down the signposted footpath, which will take you to a lane. Turning right on to this will take you down into Hollinsclough, as long as you remember to keep going downhill and turn right where the lane finishes.

Coming down into the village you have to do a bit of zigzagging. Zig left past the phone box and the Methodists and zag right, leaving Hollinsclough past the school. Follow this road due E for about 400 yds, taking the footpath on the left just after a barn.

See that craggy hill just opposite? Impressive, isn't it? You are making for the gap in between it and its neighbour to the right. The track you are on turns right after 300 yds, running due E alongside the river for some way before crossing it (into Derbyshire) and climbing slightly to the road.

The footpath simply crosses the road and carries on in the same direction, but if you've got time, the inclination or a desire to eat your sandwiches somewhere a bit special, you could turn left and head up the road a way. You can't (legally) get up the hills on either side of you, but what you can do is go through the pass between them to an extraordinary place where the ground broadens out and you are completely surrounded as if in a bowl. A delightful, still and almost (in the right conditions) magical place.

Crossing the road you begin to skirt the bulk of Parkhouse Hill (that big thing on your left), though you soon start to drop down to meet the main road. You are now heading for the large hill opposite – you are going up it.

Cross the main road, crossing the stile opposite, and start to climb up to your left, though once you near the brow of the hill the path begins to bend right, and by the time it comes down into Sterndale it is heading due E once more.

Turn right on to the road in Sterndale, past the Quiet Woman (see Walk 1 for interesting story), continuing in the same direction (signposted for Crowdecote) where the main road forks off to the left.

This road soon bends round to the right in between High Wheeldon to the right and Aldery Cliff. Actually, High Wheeldon is well worth a bit of a climb for the magnificent views from the top, but I expect you're a bit knackered by now.

Where the road starts to bend left, there's a barn on your left. Take the lane off to the right. Where, 200 yds later, this bends right towards a farm, carry straight on, crossing the Dove into Staffs. This path will bring you back to Longnor.

WALK 3: Longnor-Morridge

A walk over extremely varied countryside taking you over limestone country to the higher, bleaker moors in the west.

Moderate going, one long climb.
10½ miles, 4 hrs.
Start SK088649.

Follow Walk 2 on to the first road and turn right for 500 yds as far as Hardings Booth (opposite a road off right). Here take the footpath on the left by the side of a brook, coming out on a minor road at Shining

Ford. Turn left on to the road, cross the small bridge and take the footpath on the right after the grim-looking house on your left.

You climb gently, soon coming out at a road junction, where you want to take the road down to Newtown, carrying on in much the same direction as the footpath you have just left. After 300 yds of road, take the lane on the right past the church, bending left immediately afterwards. You are now on a path which will take you uphill on to the moor, going more or less SW for three-quarters of a mile.

This brings you to a road, where you should turn right. Three hundred yards later, take the track on the left leading up to a farm and, when it gets there, turn sharply right along the footpath which follows the wall around very gradually to your left and uphill for three-quarters of a mile.

You will now come out on to Morridge. You might care to pause for a bit of a look at the views in all directions unless, of course, it's raining and misty, in which case you might care to pause to ask yourself why you came up here on a day like this.

Turn left and you'll see a fork in the road. Take the left fork, signposted to Warslow. Except – you can't see it from here but there's a pub called the Mermaid half a mile down the road to the right. The choice is yours and it's a free country.

About 700 yds down the road to the left there's a footpath off to the left taking you downhill NE off the moor. After going through a farmyard, taking the lane out to the right of it and then bending off to the left, the path comes out on to a road near a ridiculously steep and tight corner.

Take the footpath opposite, coming out very soon on to another road and turn left. After 400 yds, take the footpath on the right to some farm buildings. Take the footpath to the left here, leading away ENE (though it bends a bit) and a mile and a bit later this will bring you out on a bend in the Longnor road.

Turn left and climb uphill to the left bend at the top, and take the footpath on the right down a small valley (and a very muddy one) to the road on the other side. Turn right and 200 yds later take the footpath on the left down to a farm. Go past the farm and cross the bridge over the river.

On the other side, take the lane to the left and, after 300 yds, turn left again at an overgrown stone stile. This footpath takes you right back to Longnor.

WALK 4: Longnor-Pool-Fawfieldhead

A charming riverside walk leading to upland farmland with excellent views of the surrounding moorland.

Easy going with no substantial climbing.
5½ miles, 2 hrs.
Start SK088649.

Going E out of the market place (right from facing the craft centre), pass the Cheshire Cheese and take the next footpath on the right, opposite a squarish Georgian tenement building with the numbers six and seven on the doors.

Go left through the farmyard at the bottom, taking the footpath downhill at the other side of it. At the riverbank, turn left. You bend away from the river slightly, crossing numerous small streams and, after one-and-a-half miles, come to a stile over a stone wall into a green lane. Take the lane on the right, bringing you back down to the river and over a footbridge.

Over the river, take the right hand of the two tracks, going uphill through a farmyard. Immediately after the farm, take the signposted footpath on the right through two fields to a minor road. Turn right here.

Three hundred yards later take the footpath on the left downhill to a footbridge over the boggy little stream and, climbing uphill again, come out on to another road, this time the main Longnor-Warslow road. You come out on a tight bend, and the road is often used as part of the course for the North Staffs Breakneck Idiot Lobotomised Daredevil Driving-Too-Fast-But-I-Don't-Care championships which are always in progress, so do be careful.

Turn left and head downhill until the road bends off to the left. Take the footpath on the right. Alright, one of the footpaths on the right, for there are several. The one you need goes past the little house, right over a stile immediately afterwards and then directly uphill at right angles to the stream at the bottom of the hill. This is where the panoramas of moor-topped hills begin to open out all around you, but especially behind you.

This will bring you past a farmhouse, on to a track coming out on to a road. Turn left on to the road, past a footpath sign and a sympathetically constructed new house to a junction. Turn right here.

Two hundred yards later, take the footpath on the right leading downhill at 45 degrees from the road. This is waymarked all the way down to the bottom of the hill at Heath House. When you get there turn right on to the road and this brings you back to Longnor.

Below Hollins Cross (Castleton)

Knotbury Lee Farm

Turn Edge △

Wicken Walls

GRADBACH
Car Park Manor Farm

Lud's Church
(Cave) Gradbach

Sniddles Head Farm

Paddock

Goldstich
Moss

Bearstone Rock

N

Hazel Barrow

The Roaches

△

Rockhall

·—·—·—·— walk 1
· · · · · · · ·walk 2
— — — — — walk 3

0   1 mile

THE WEST

GRADBACH

There isn't a village, as such, at Gradbach, just a scattering of farms, some hills, a youth hostel and a car park. Lying between the A53 and the A54 south-west of Buxton, it's in the wildest and most desolate (you can walk here without seeing a single person, even in summer) part of Staffordshire, but only just – the river on the other side of the Peak District National Park car park from the road marks the Cheshire county boundary.

WALK 1: Gradbach-The Roaches

A walk over dramatic upland pasture, moorland and a fine rocky ridge, descending into a planted, but charming, forest.

Moderate going with climbing.
7 miles, 3 hrs.
Start SK998663.

Turn left out of the car park on to the road. Almost immediately, take the footpath on the right up the bank, bringing you to some farm buildings. Behind these there is a stile over the fence and the footpath continues uphill.

Once approaching the top, pass a ruined farmhouse and bend slightly left, pass a weird rock formation and a second ruin and turn more definitely left, going around the top of the hill but not losing any height yet. There are lots of good sandwich spots up here, but, agonisingly, it is far too early to stop.

Coming around the brow of the hill you should now be able to see Sniddles Head Farm below you and to the left. Aim for the track to the left of the farm, which brings you out on to the road.

At the road, turn right and continue to the bend, where the path signposted to Roach End goes straight on and slightly downhill. Follow this down to the bottom of the hill, then bear left towards the farm.

Arriving there, keep to the left of the farm and beyond it go between the two barns and head past the old farmhouse you can see at some distance further on.

The most direct route here would be to cross Shaw Bottom over to your right, but the gate through which the path goes bears the legend 'Walkers Keep Out'. We can justifiably conclude from this that the farmer at Shaw Bottom is not keen on walkers crossing his land and, since there is no public right of way, we have to take a detour, following the footpath to the road.

Turn right on the road and, at the corner, turn right again on to the minor road. When this forks, go right. Cross the stream (though you may not recognise it as such) and pass under some overhead power lines. There is soon a track on the left over a cattle-grid, which you should take. Keep heading S or SW, noting the view of Ramshaw Rocks to your left until the track bends down to a farm on the left and there is a stile in front of you, which you should cross.

This path gradually bends around to the right until, all of a sudden, there is a spectacular view of the Roaches and the Staffordshire countryside beyond. That large expanse of water, by the way, is the reservoir at Rudyard, whose name Rudyard Kipling was given as he was conceived there (honestly. What a shame it wasn't Wildboarclough). Just as you get level with the line of the ridge, take the path on the right climbing up it bringing you, eventually, to the highest point. This is a glorious bit of walking, and it's not usually too crowded, except for the rock climbers and once you are on the top you can safely ignore them.

After the trig point at the end of the ridge, follow the path down to the bend in the road underneath Bearstone Rock. When you get there, turn around and see if you can figure out why it's named after a bear since, of all the animals it might bear some resemblance to, the one it bears least to is a bear. Maybe Bearstone Rock was simply thought to be a better name than the more accurate but less romantic Amoebastone Rock.

There is a footpath opposite and a sign saying Lower Roach End No Parking. Go over the first stile then turn right, going over another stile on to a path taking you sharply downhill past the aforementioned Lower Roach End. This brings you into Gradbach Wood. It is possible to lose your path here, but if you keep the stream to your right you can't go far wrong.

Eventually you come to a footbridge over the stream to your right, and the path past the Youth Hostel and back to the car park takes you over this and by the riverbank.

WALK 2: Gradbach-Lud's Church-Roach End-Goldstitch Moss

A tremendous variety of scenery is to be had in these five miles: riverbank, woodland, a ridgewalk and open moorland. Add to this Lud's Church, an interesting natural cleft in the rocks, and you have a compelling little walk.

Easy going with long, gentle climbs.
5½ miles, 2½ hrs.
Start SJ998663.

Turn right out of Gradbach car park on to the road. Go down, 300 yds later, to the right into the Youth Hostel grounds, round the building (itself not without interest, being a converted mill) and up the bank on the other side.

Follow the riverbank, home to many waterbirds including kingfishers, until you come to the footbridge taking you into Gradbach Wood. On the other side the footpath is well waymarked, being signposted to Swythamley and Lud's Church.

Follow it uphill through the wood until you come to the path on the left to Lud's Church. This is only a few hundred yards long, but the trip to this peculiar cleft in the rocks does involve coming back the same way so you can miss it out if you want to. It is worth going to see though, particularly if you happen to be a fan of medieval English literature – Lud's Church has associations with *Sir Gawain and the Green Knight* as well as strong folkloric connections of its own.

Having poked about in the cave, make your way back to the original path and continue to the left out of the trees and on to the open hillside. This path soon crosses a wall and starts to bend round to the left, eventually climbing slightly and then dropping down on the other side of the brow of the hill.

Where it meets another track coming from the right, just before a wall, turn left, and climb uphill on to the shoulder of the hill, climbing about 300 feet to the road at Roach End. If you haven't been up there before, it may be worth considering nipping up the hill in front of you as the views from the top of it are a bit on the commanding side, but our route takes us to the left, down the track to Lower Roach End.

Going past the house, follow the track downhill and to the right as it comes to meet and crosses Black Brook. Where a well-defined track bends off to the left some 300 yds later, you should be able to see stiles turning half left, away from the stream, gently uphill. Follow these out into the expansive rough pasture of Goldstitch Moss, and then turn left, heading N, uphill to meet the road coming from the right as it bends suddenly northwards.

At the road, carry on in the same direction (N) for 300 yds until you come to a farm track on the left which takes you to a stile on the right before the farm and up Gradbach Hill. It is easy to lose the path here, but the trick is to aim diagonally uphill NE (i.e. at 45 degrees to the road) until you're over the brow, and then make for the ruined farmhouse to your left and from there follow the remains of its lane downhill past a rock outcrop and into a large rough pasture. The stile at the other side of this leads you down to a farm, on the other side of which is the path bringing you down to the road where the car park is 100 yds on the left.

WALK 3: Gradbach-Turn Edge-Wolf Edge-Flash-Far Brook

A walk over some of the desolate and beautiful moorland in the western Peak District.

Moderate-hard going with a lot of climbing.
5½ miles, 3 hrs.
Start SJ998663.

Turn left out of the car park to the junction with the road. Turn left here, then take the footpath on the right which climbs away steeply uphill.

In fact, you continue going uphill for the best part of three-quarters of a mile, eventually turning left on to a track right under Turn Edge. Follow this as it bends round to the right, taking the footpath on the right up through a bunch of trees 400 yds later.

This takes you over Turn Edge – it can be extremely squishy up here. You are now making for a lane to the left of the group of farm buildings you can see ahead of you to the right. Coming out on to the lane, turn right and follow it round and downhill past the farm, coming to a T-junction.

Turn left here, taking the footpath on the right 150 yds later, crossing the small stream via a footbridge. Climb uphill at right-angles to the road you just left, coming to a lane just over the brow of the hill, where you should turn right and follow it down into the village of Flash.

Do try to resist the impulse to call it 'Flash . . . Aa-aaahhh', though this is very hard to do. Emerging on to the road, the main bulk of the village (it calls itself the highest village in England, though what they get high on around here is anyone's guess) is to your left, so turn right, ignoring it completely.

In a short while, this road will begin to descend steeply. After 600 yds turn right up the entrance to a farm, following the track left of the farm buildings. Bending round to the right, cross a footbridge and take the path on the left. Where, after 500 yds and a slight descent, this path meets the corner of a lane, turn right for 400 yds until you meet the path you came up that first hill on. Thought it looked a bit familiar? Turn left and descend to the road and car park.

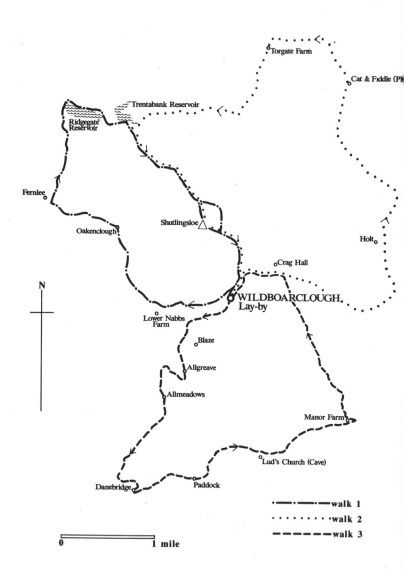

WILDBOARCLOUGH

Lots of cloughs, no wild boars, but a good pub and a lot of fine walking country is what you'll find here. This is where the Peak's Western Moors are at their wildest. The village, such as it is, is dominated by the conical bulk of Shuttingsloe, the last big hill to the west. All the walks start from the Crag Inn – there is a car park, well a lay-by, on the south side of the road a couple of hundred yards south-west of the pub.

WALK 1: Wildboarclough-Macclesfield Forest-Shuttingsloe

A walk through open moorland, upland pasture and forest plantation, this walk has scenery which can be bleak or lush, depending on the season. It also offers a reasonably easy way of getting at some of Cheshire's wildest country.

Moderate, occasionally hard going, one strenuous climb.
7½ miles, 3 hrs.
Start SJ982684.

Take the footpath uphill just left of the Crag Inn, following it as it turns west over the lower reaches of Shuttingsloe, meeting a farm track after three-quarters of a mile and coming down to meet the road.

Turn right on the road as far as Greenway Bridge (250 yds), here taking the footpath to the right on the right-hand side of the brook which runs under the bridge. Follow it for 350 yds until the stream forks, then bend left over a footbridge, following the right side of the left fork in the stream (if you're still with me).

This takes you to a farm. Turn left here on the farm track until it bends, heading straight on the footpath across the field to a second track, which leads you W to a road.

The Hanging Gate is directly opposite. Ignore temptation and venture ye not into that den of shame, for, verily, thou hast a long and arduous journey ahead of thee. Besides, there's another pub further on.

Nip down the track at the back of the car park, taking you NW across fields to another road. Go left and take the signposted footpath on the right 150 yds later, just before the phone box. This is the Gritstone Trail, for what it's worth.

Follow it for just over half a mile until you are virtually in Macclesfield Forest. You can tell when you are almost in Macclesfield Forest because there are a lot of trees. Shortly after a building on your right, the trail forks off left and a lane carries straight on (N), into the forest. Go this way.

You will shortly notice Ridgegate Reservoir on your right. Big wet thing, right? Then you'll come to a road and, bless my soul, there's a pub. The Leather's Smithy. This is the official halfway point, so you can go in if you want.

If not, turn right and follow the road down the side of the reservoir. Six hundred yards later you'll come to a junction. Turn left, past the car park and visitors' centre with toilets, helpful maps and tray of free leaflets (empty). Another 200 yds on, take the signposted footpath on the right. This is well waymarked and leads out of the forest, over Shuttingsloe and back to Wildboarclough.

As you approach the top of the hill, by the way, you are offered a choice of routes. The path crosses a wall and bends right, following it all the way to the top, though there is a less strenuous route carrying straight on. It's worth going to the top.

Coming down into Wildboarclough you meet a wood and a lane. Take the lane downhill (due S) for 500 yds, turning right where it meets the road. This brings you back to the Crag.

WALK 2: Wildboarclough-Daneblower-Cat and Fiddle-Macclesfield Forest

A moorland walk which can be quite taxing, despite the fact that it follows marked paths. In wet weather the going can be a lot harder, and it can turn into one of those perversely fun gruelling slogs which make the cup of tea/pint of beer at the end the best you've ever tasted.

Hard-moderate going with climbs.
10½ miles, 5 hrs.
Start SJ982684.

Head back towards Wildboarclough past the Crag Inn and turn right on the road, climbing uphill until you come to a three-way junction. Take the road sightly right, still climbing for another 200 yds until the road bends right. Here take the lane off to the left. This leads to a path which climbs uphill and meets the main road 500 yds later.

Cross the road, taking the footpath on the other side. Over the next stile, bend slightly left as a clough starts to open out beneath you, and make for a group of farm buildings ahead of you to the left.

This brings you out on a (very) minor road. Take the track opposite and slightly right, beneath the crown of Cutthorn Hill. This brings you, when the track starts to bend left, to Three Shires Head, the place where the valley forks and Derbyshire, Staffordshire and Cheshire meet. I expect they're planning to nip out for a pint later.

Take the valley on the left, staying on the left of the stream and heading NNW for 200 yds then due N. Once you've crossed some old dry-stone walls, the stream makes a major right turn. Follow it a little way then strike uphill slightly left, crossing another wall before meeting an old quarry track. Cross this to meet the road uphill another 100 feet.

Over the road there's a footpath signposted to the Cat and Fiddle. Follow it. You will come, a mile or so later, to the Cat and Fiddle. Turn left here, following the main road for 200 yds, then follow the old road on the right where the new one bends left, rejoining it some 500 yds later.

Carry on for another 100 yds then take the turning on the left towards Macclesfield Forest. Follow this road for half a mile until you pass a farm on the left. Just past it, cross the stile on the left on to a footpath bringing you back in front of the farmhouse to the farm lane.

Turn right here and follow the lane over the crest of the hill and down to meet Clough Brook on the left. Crossing the brook will bring you on to a farm track, and following this downhill takes you on to a minor road.

Here you can shorten the walk by turning left on to the road and following it back one-and-a-half miles to Wildboarclough. This also misses out the last big climb.

Otherwise, having turned left on to the road, almost immediately double back on yourself, taking the fork on the right, signposted to Macclesfield Forest. At the next junction head straight on, towards Langley. Follow this road for a mile, taking the footpath on the left once you can see Trentabank Reservoir through the trees to your right. This takes you over Shuttingsloe and back to Wildboarclough, as in Walk 1.

WALK 3: Wildboarclough-Allgreave-Wincle-Gradbach

A walk which is slightly more gentle in character than the previous two (and which passes a couple of fine pubs), though it does have its share of climbing.

Moderate going, two long climbs.
9 miles, 4 hrs.
Start SJ982684.

Head SW away from the Crag Inn. Take the small lane off to the left after 500 yds, crossing the brook, and taking the footpath on the right immediately afterwards. This runs parallel to the road for a few hundred yards before joining a farm track and bending away uphill to the left.

Stay with the track as it bends slightly right and then joins a more well-defined, but somewhat overgrown, lane. Turn left on to this, which will bring you down on to the A54 at Allgreave. There is no village to speak of, though the Rose and Crown is a good pub.

Turn right on to the road, past the pub (far too early), round the bend and down the hill. After the bridge, take the turning on the left, and follow this road for 500 yds. Take the signposted footpath on the left at the second farm on the left (Allmeadows), where the road bends right.

The path follows the farm track slightly downhill before bending left (SW) to run parallel to the River Dane, which you can see downhill to your left. Simply follow the path SW and it will bring you out in Wincle, just to the right of the Ship.

Turn left and follow the road as it winds through Wincle and into Danebridge. At this point (if not before), you will realise that Danebridge is so called because it is built around a bridge over the River Dane. Ingenious.

At this point there are also two route options. The footpath on the left just over the bridge (signposted to Gradbach) follows the river all the way and makes for pleasant, easy walking. It's more rewarding, however, to take the second footpath on the left, 75 yds later, also signposted to Gradbach.

This turns sharply left and climbs uphill, turning left on to a cart track at the back of Hangingstone Farm. Follow the path past another set of buildings on your right, turning left where it forks 200 yds later.

This leads you over the crest of the hill and down into Gradbach Wood. It is possible to lose your way here as it is not always easy to tell which is the proper track. As a rule, though, keep heading due E, and you will come to a footbridge over a brook joining the Dane from the SE.

Cross this and take the path by the riverside, heading NE. This takes you through the grounds of the Youth Hostel (a converted silk mill, from the days when Macclesfield was a centre of that industry) and on to a metalled lane.

Just past the National Park car park on your left, take the footpath on the left, crossing the river and following the right bank of a brook to the road ahead of you.

Turn left here, following the road around a ridiculous bend. Just where it starts to go back on itself, take the signposted footpath on the right, climbing sharply uphill to the left of a wall. The path is quite well marked and takes you over some rough ground to a minor road almost 200 feet higher up the hillside.

Cross the road and continue climbing up what is now (for a while) a farm track. It soon becomes an indistinct footpath again, and veers right slightly, though there are gate-stiles to aim for. It goes right to the very top of the hill, becoming easier to follow as it descends the other side, leading NNW to the A54.

Where the path emerges, take the minor road to Wildboarclough opposite, turning left at the top and then left again past the Crag Inn.

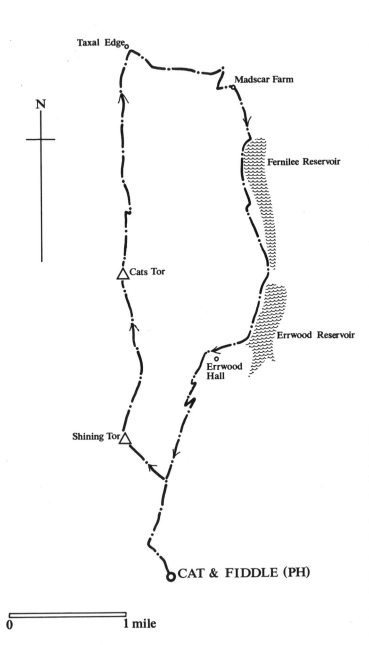

CAT AND FIDDLE

A pub in the middle of nowhere may seem bizarre to modern folk, but it's a relic of coaching days when it wasn't possible to traverse the entire country in one day. Even today, there are occasions when this pub on the A537 Buxton-Macclesfield is a very welcome sight. After a long walk over the moors, for instance . . . Car parking is available opposite the pub.

WALK 1: Cat and Fiddle-Shining Tor-Taxal Edge-Shooter's Clough

An excellent, and varied, moorland walk, with lowland sections.

Moderate and occasionally hard going, two hard climbs.
11 miles, 5 hrs.
Start SK001719.

Facing the pub on the road, turn left and follow the road for 250 yds, taking the footpath on the right (the old road). As a clough appears in front of you, turn right at a wall and head NNW along the side of the clough.

Climb the next stile and, 300 yds later if you haven't drowned in the peat bog, take the signposted footpath on the left up that big hill in front of you. At the trig point take the footpath on the right and follow it along the long ridge. The wall on your left is the Derbyshire-Cheshire border.

At weekends it can get a little crowded up here with people flying model aeroplanes, walking dogs and children, the reason for this being that there is a car park at the other end of the ridge where a road crosses it. Never mind.

At the aforementioned road, turn right and almost immediately take the footpath on the left across a heather-covered area to another road, at which point turn right and follow the road for half a mile.

Take the (signposted) footpath on the right just before Windgather Rocks, turning right at the next wall down towards the plantation. Skirt its W perimeter for 300 yds, then turn right into the trees, descending a clough then climbing the other side (it can be slippery here).

Emerging from the trees, go downhill due E to the lane. Cross it and take the footpath directly opposite, down a broad farm lane. Past the farm, going downhill, take the lane on the right, bending left over a stream, making your way due S on the other side to the reservoir.

By the side of the dam, the path splits. Go left, taking the path into the trees by the side of the reservoir, due S. In the plantation, though this is an artificial landscape, it is possible to be astonished by the beauty of what you see – one February, with spots of melting snow on the ground, we came through here and the ground was carpeted with rust-red decayed pine needles which contrasted vividly with the green of the lichen growing on the walls and the white of the snow.

This footpath takes you S through the plantation for a mile. You emerge on to a road by a dam. Take the road on the right to a T-junction, then turn left. Follow this road for half a mile until, just before Shooter's Clough Bridge, taking the footpath on the right (part of a nature trail and waymarked) which climbs steeply up steps. This passes between rhododendrons and other plants which mark the area out as having been part of the estate of Errwood Hall, whose ruins you can glimpse through the trees to your left further up the hill.

The footpath emerges into a clearing, swinging around SW before passing along a lane and descending to cross a brook. Here, climb the opposite bank to another track and turn left, briefly, before taking the next footpath on the right by the side of another brook.

After 400 yds, cross the brook to the left and start climbing, zigzagging your way to the top where, crossing a stile, turn right on to a path which will take you up the shoulder of the hill and back to the footpath to the Cat and Fiddle, passing the turn-off to Shining Tor you made at the beginning.

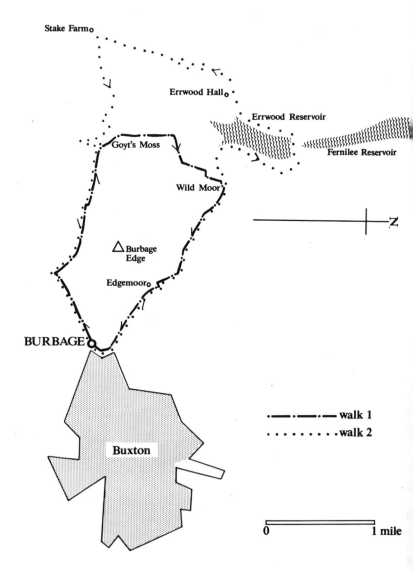

BUXTON

A nice town, though sadly lacking in the nice pub department, Buxton is an extraordinarily well-placed base for the hill-walking city-dweller. It has delicatessens, supermarkets, a cheese shop, banks, building societies, tourist amenities and off-licences, and yet there are high hills and wild moors a mile away.

These walks start from Burbage, once a village but now part of the town (one might say, a suburbage) on the A53 Macclesfield road. Car drivers can park there, though it is perfectly possible to walk from the centre of town.

WALK 1: Burbage-Goyt's Moss-Wild Moor

A short, but exhilarating, walk on to the moor.

Moderate going (harder in wet weather) with one long steep climb.
5½ miles, 2½ hrs.
Start SK044728.

Starting from Macclesfield Old Road (there is now a smart new Macclesfield road because this one was too hard for the poor little modern car), walk to the farm at the end of the road and take the footpath on the right, by the side of the wood.

Over the other side of the hill, the path leads into a clough descending steeply towards the road at the bottom of Goyt's Clough. This can get very squishy and slippery in wet weather.

At the bottom follow the path which runs to the right parallel to the road, either striking off to the right slightly when the road bends away to the left, heading uphill and due N to a wall, or following the path to the wall. Either way, turn right at the wall, uphill, until it falls away to the left, then follow it around.

Follow the wall around right-angled right and left bends, crossing the next wall you come to and descending to the bottom of a clough. Climb the other side and take the footpath on the right up the left side of the clough.

Where the clough splits, 700 yds later, strike sharply uphill between the two branches, heading ESE. You will cross the remains of an old mineral railway (with its filled-in tunnel to your right) and follow the left side of a wall almost to the top, striking off right over a stile. Descend through the trees to a lane, turning right and following it back S then SE to Burbage.

WALK 2: Burbage-Wild Moor-Shooter's Clough-Goyt's Moss

Covering some of the same territory as Walk 1, this is a harder, more strenuous outing, though it also offers a far greater variety of scenery – moor, plantation, rhododendron gardens – though, of course, mainly moor.

Moderate and hard going, two long hard climbs.
10 miles, 5 hrs.
Start SK044728.

The walk starts on Bishop's Lane, heading straight as a die NW out of Burbage. At the end go between the gateposts of the Edgemoor estate, and follow the lane past the buildings and around to the right. Shortly after this, take the footpath on the left, sharply uphill, at the edge of a plantation.

This takes you over the top of the hill and down a clough on the other side. Follow the path all the way to the bottom and as it swings right near the reservoir.

This brings you to the road near Bunsal Cob, a strange blob of a hillock. Turn left and cross the dam and, on the other side, follow the road left. At the T-junction, turn left and follow the road by the side of the reservoir for half a mile.

Where the trees come down to meet the road from the right, just before Shooter's Clough Bridge (which you can see), take the footpath on the right into the old Errwood Estate. The path climbs steeply uphill but, since it was made part of a nature trail in the 60s, is stepped. Whether this makes it any easier is debateable. Amuse yourself by reading the explanatory notices nailed up on posts.

This does not last long. Soon the path bends left, into a clearing (at certain times of the year you can sort of make out the ruins of the hall below you to the left), goes through some more trees and crosses a brook.

You then meet a track running across your path, take it to the left then quickly take the path off to the right. This starts to climb steeply, and zigzags twice before crossing a stile, some 400 feet higher, on to a broad path running alongside a wall. Take this to the right.

Follow this for almost a mile, past the broad path to the right up Shining Tor, until you come to a stile over a high wall. Cross this and take the path on the left, downhill, for a mile.

Where the path emerges from the trees, near the bottom, follow it around to the right and make your way down to the road. Turn left and take the next footpath on the right, crossing the footbridge and taking the footpath steeply up the clough.

Follow this to the top of the hill, until you come to a wood, then follow it to the right to a lane. Turn left and follow this back to Burbage.

Below Hollins Cross (Castleton)

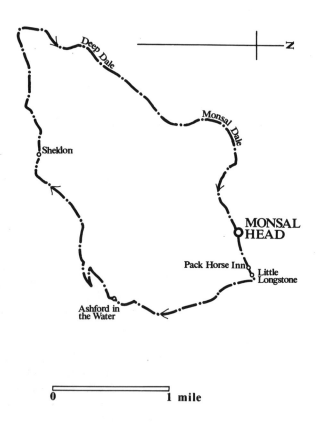

Deep Dale

Monsal Dale

Sheldon

MONSAL HEAD

Pack Horse Inn

Little Longstone

Ashford in the Water

0   1 mile

CENTRAL

MONSAL DALE

It can get a little crowded, but there again the scenery is undeniably spectacular. The curious steep but straight sides of the dale make it look almost artificial, but also render it highly distinctive. There are two fine pubs in the vicinity – the Stable at Monsal Head and the tiny but excellent Packhorse in Little Longstone. The walk starts from the car park at Monsal Head on the B6465 between Wardlow and Ashford.

WALK 1: Monsal Head-Ashford-Sheldon-Deep Dale-Monsal Dale

Not only do you get to explore Monsal Dale, you also cross examples of just about every kind of scenery the limestone Peak has to offer.

Moderate going with one hard section, one hard climb.
8 miles, 3½ hrs.
Start SK815716.

Cross the main road and make for Little Longstone, going downhill past the Packhorse. Shortly afterwards take the footpath on the right (there are two, take the one at right-angles to the road) over fields SSE to the old railway.

Climb up on to the railway and take the footpath opposite and left, which continues SSE over more fields. Cross a minor road and take the footpath opposite, keeping to the left-hand edge of the field.

At the next road, again take the footpath opposite, uphill, cutting across a paddock on to another road. Turn left and follow this, past some new houses built in traditional materials, into Ashford. At the fork in the road turn right, past the vicarage (is there still a gasmask in the upstairs window?) to another fork and turn right again.

This leads you down to the A6. Cross the road and turn left, pausing, if it is autumn, to admire the brilliant red vines on the wall of the house on the corner (it looks less attractive at other times of the year).

Take the next road on the right and follow it for 250 yds until it bends left, and then take the footpath on the right. A short way into the field there are three distinct paths. Which one do you fancy? Bad luck. The one you need is the one on the left, the one which goes straight uphill. It's quite a climb, particularly if the weather is hot, close, or wet (and when is it anything else?). The views, however, make it worthwhile. Almost.

Having kept left of the woods, you find yourself uphill from a sewage farm. Descend gradually to the bottom of the small valley and continue on to the road, turning right once you are over the stile.

This is Sheldon, an old lead-mining village with some very old houses, a church but, cruelly, no pub. Some of the houses, if you look closely, have witch-steps on their window-lintels (little ledges which stick out from the wall for witches to land on – stops them coming into the house, apparently).

Climb through and out of the village, following the road round to the left on the other side. Take the second footpath on the right, just before a barn on the left side of the road. Confusingly, this doesn't follow the track, but swings left of that small stone construction in front of you. There are, however, stiles to aim for.

It brings you out on to a long straight road. Turn right for 100 yds, then take the signposted footpath on the right, down a lane into Deep Dale. Once you have crossed the stile into the dale proper, keep to the bottom of the dale but go through the iron gate on to the other (right) side of the wall.

You descend for almost three-quarters of a mile, the dale getting deeper and steeper and finally wooded. Where you approach a rocky outcrop the path forks. The official right of way (denoted here by little yellow arrows) goes off to the right, but it is infinitely more fun (though a little dangerous, especially in the wet), to keep straight on and take the steeply-plunging rocky path along the dale bottom.

Once it starts to broaden out and level off, follow the path along the left side of the dale to the car park on the A6 – you will be able to hear the traffic on the road by now. Turn left into the car park and go through the gap in the hedge on to the road. Cross the road (you are on a bend, so be careful) and take the footpath opposite.

Where this path forks 100 yds later, take the path on the right, along the dale bottom. The dale bends through a massive, mile-long right-handed, right-angled bend. You entered the dale heading N. When you're heading E, look for a fork in the path and head along the riverbank to a metal footbridge. Cross this and take the footpath which climbs, comparatively gently, to the left and back to Monsal Head.

The foot of Cavedale (Castleton)

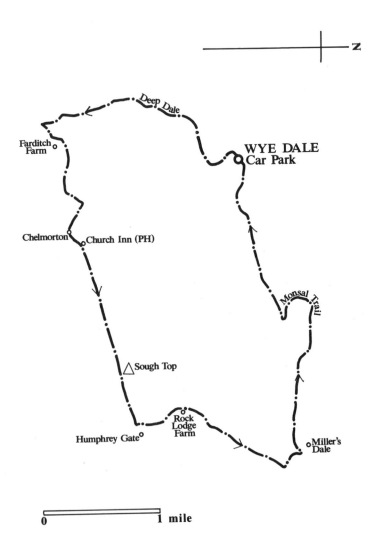

WYEDALE

Wyedale, where the A6 runs east of Buxton, would contain some pretty spectacular countryside, were it not for the damage wrought by quarries, the railway and, not least, the road itself. However, all is not lost – a little way from the road there is some beautiful, and not often visited scenery.

WALK 1: Deep Dale-Chelmorton-Taddington-Miller's Dale

Four dales and three beautiful little villages feature in this walk. It starts from the Wyedale car park on the A6.

Easy going with one difficult section, one climb.
10 miles, 4 hrs.
Start SK103726.

From the car park, cross the road and take the footpath opposite and to the right, running alongside Topley Pike Quarry. This bit of the walk looks horrible, but it is a reminder that quarrying is still one of the Peak's biggest earners. You could try walking with your eyes shut, though considerations of safety would tend to weigh against this.

After a few hundred yards you leave the quarry behind and the dale – Deep Dale – becomes what it once was all along its length, a steep-sided, wooded gorge. Follow it for almost a mile, until it splits.

Take the dale on the left, Horseshoe Dale, heading a few degrees E of S. Half a mile later, where the dale bends left, follow the path up the bank opposite you, emerging on to a major road, and turn left.

Three hundred yards later, there used to be a footpath on the left, though it was recently displaced by work being done. If it has been restored, use it to cut out the corner in the road, bending right across two fields. Otherwise, follow the road round the left bend (i.e. not going down the Chelmorton turn-off).

There is then a right bend (where the path should emerge) followed by another left. On the left bend, take the footpath on the right, down an overgrown lane which continues along the line of the road. Follow this over a stile to a wall, where it turns left into a lane and heads NE to a road. Turn right on the road into Chelmorton.

In the village turn left, and head uphill. You pass the Church Inn (so called so that you could legitimately say 'I'm off to church' and go for a few jars. Also because it's close to the church), and follow the lane until it finishes.

Take the lane on the right, climbing sharply uphill, and follow it until it meets another lane. Here take the footpath opposite and to the right, heading ENE across fields and hugging the right-hand side of a long, straight wall. This moor is covered with prehistoric sites, including a chambered cairn at Fivewells, two fields N of the farm you pass on the right.

This footpath brings you to a lane into Taddington. Turn left and follow it through the west side of the village (though it is worth turning right at the main street, into the village, to explore). Follow the lane under the A6, and for a further three-quarters of a mile around a long right-hand bend, to the hamlet of Priestcliffe.

Where the lane splits, take the lane going off due N, ever-so-slightly left. After 100 yds, once the buildings on the left have finished, take the footpath on the right at the corner of a field, heading NE. After half a mile, this bends left and descends into Miller's Dale through some trees. On the way down the slope, you meet the old railway line which is now the Monsal Trail. Turn left.

Follow this back to the car park (about three miles). The section which goes through Chee Dale, though spectacular to look at, can be rather slippery in wet weather as it involves making your way over smooth rocks by the river where the railway goes through a tunnel which is unsafe. This stretch is also very popular with rock climbers, which is another disadvantage.

Conies Dale (Peak Forest)

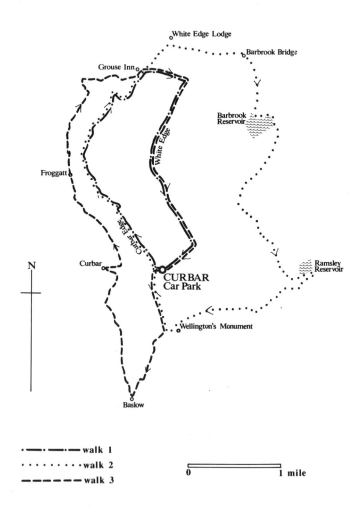

White Edge Lodge

Barbrook Bridge

Grouse Inn

Barbrook
Reservoir

White Edge

Froggatt

Curbar Edge

Curbar

CURBAR
Car Park

Ramsley
Reservoir

Wellington's Monument

N

Baslow

—·—·—·— walk 1
············ walk 2
— — — — — walk 3

0   1 mile

CURBAR

Not much to report about Curbar – it's a pleasant enough little village, though it is now as much a base for people who commute to Sheffield as it is a genuine village, but these things happen. Far more worrying for the discerning walker are the huge numbers of rock climbers who hang about the environs – the edges above Curbar to the east are among the most popular climbing sites in the country.

Walks 1, 2 and 3 start from the car park half a mile along the lane out of the village to the east.

WALK 1: Curbar-Froggat Edge-Grouse Inn-White Edge

This is an easy walk, but you get a great feel for the East Moors. They may not be all that high but they are, depending on the season and the conditions, dramatic and attractive. There is a varity of wildlife in the summer, and in the winter, if you manage to come at a time when the climbers are not out in force, the sense of isolation and grandeur can be quite awesome, even though you are never too far from civilisation.

Moderate going, one gentle climb.
6 miles, 2½ hrs.
Start SK263747.

Take the footpath N out of the car park. It follows the top of the edge, and, as you look down to your left a magnificent panorama of the Derwent Valley opens up. The path is well defined and easy to follow, and leads you two miles later to the B6054 north of Froggat.

Coming out on to the road, turn right and follow it round a large, sweeping left bend. When the road straightens out again you will be able to see the Grouse Inn ahead of you to the left.

Just past the Grouse (or having nipped into it if there are not too many climbers about – they do tend to congregate in there and their conversations about scaling overhangs with both hands tied behind their backs, blindfolded and playing the ukulele can be both tedious and vexing at the same time), take the footpath to the right NE on to White Edge Moor.

This climbs gently and leads you to the open country. Stay on the path until it meets another running left and right, and turn right on to it. This path follows White Edge practically the whole way back to the car park. If you look to the right you will be able to see the path you took along the top of Curbar and Froggat Edges below you.

The path takes you past a trig point and, 400 yds later, forks. Fork right, and you will find yourself emerging on to the road just a little way east of the car park (i.e. turn right and there you are).

WALK 2: Curbar-Grouse Inn-Bar Brook-Ramsley-Eaglestone

An extension of Walk 1, exploring more of the rugged East Moor and passing many prehistoric sites along the way.

Moderate going, one gentle climb.
10 miles, 4 hrs.
Start SK263747.

Follow Walk 1 as far as the Grouse Inn, taking the second footpath on the right, beside a National Trust signpost. After 300 yds, this path meets another: turn right and head a little way S of E (about 100 degrees) uphill and over the rocky area that marks the edge of White Edge Moor.

Stay on this bearing for half a mile, until you come to Lady's Cross – a neolithic rampart – where you should bend slightly left and make for the road at Barbrook Bridge.

About 75 yds before the road, take the footpath on the right, parallel to it, for 300 yds, until it meets a wide track. Turn right and follow the track to Barbrook Reservoir. This is great walking country – it's wild and yet easy going, there are curlews and other moorland birds and there are wild flowers if you know where to look and it's the right time of year. Why don't you find a sheltered spot, sit awhile, eat your sandwiches and just contemplate the absolute perfection of it? Because it's freezing, blowing a gale and chucking it down in buckets, that's why. But it could be nice up here, honest.

At the reservoir, skirt the northern side, heading S past the pumping station thingy when you've run out of water. The track runs on for another mile and a bit, and then brings you out on the Sheffield road.

When you reach it, cross it. Opposite and to the right, slightly, there's another path. Follow this to Ramsley Reservoir. It looks, you will find, remarkably similar to the last one. Squarish, wettish, that kind of thing. Skirt the south side of the reservoir, turning right at the end of it to come out on a minor road.

On the road turn right once more. After 600 yds you'll be back on the Sheffield road. Turn left and make for the crossroads, at which point turn right along the minor road signposted to Curbar (you started in Curbar, so that must be the right direction).

You can simply follow this road back to the car park, but it is infinitely more interesting, romantic and, well, just better, to take the footpath on the left after 75 yds. It's a well-defined track which heads W then SW across beautiful boulder-strewn moorland.

After three-quarters of a mile the path bends right and forks. Fork with it to the right. You'll go past the Eagle Stone (on your right. You see if you can work out why it's called the Eagle Stone. Maybe it had an eagle sitting on it once), and, half a mile later, emerge opposite the car park.

WALK 3: Curbar-Baslow-Froggat-White Edge

A walk which explores both the Derwent Valley, with its abundant natural woodlands, and its dramatic eastern edge, with rocky cliffs bounding high wild moorland.

Moderate going, one long climb.
9½ miles, 4 hrs.
Start SK263747.

Take the footpath S from the car park (on the other side of the road) signposted to Baslow. It goes S for half a mile then meets another path. Turn right here, heading SSW downhill into the village.

This brings you on to a lane leading into Baslow. The lane becomes metalled, and then the houses start. When you reach a small village green take the next lane (Gorse Bank Lane) on the right. (Turning left would take you into the village proper, and it is worth spending some time exploring Baslow as parts of it are decidedly attractive.)

This lane heads due N for half a mile, past Gorse Bank Farm before bending first left and then right, to end up heading NNE and then forking. Take the right fork into Curbar village.

You will emerge on the main village road. Take the road opposite (the Green) and follow it as it bends round to the left. After 300 yds, take the footpath on the right between a modern rancho-style bungalow called Shercroft and a house called Warren Cottage.

This path heads due E for 400 yds. Then turn left on a path which heads N, parallel to the Edge above you. It soon bends to the left and heads into the woods on the hillside – Bee Wood, it's called. This is real woodland, with real trees, and you might pause to reflect how nice it is not to be staring at rows and rows of regimented pines.

There is almost a mile of this; then you come out on to a bend in the Froggat road. Turn right and follow the road N, past the Chequers Inn. After 300 yds, take the signposted footpath on the left, downhill through some woods and on to a back-street. Turn right and walk another 300 yds, taking the next footpath on the left at a big wooden gate.

This takes you N then NE through more woods, for three-quarters of a mile before the path bends left, the woods start to thin out, and then the path forks. Take the right fork, due N, and then follow it round to the right as it follows the perimeter of the wood, climbing steeply uphill due E. After another three-quarters of a mile, this brings you out on to the road near the Grouse Inn. Turn left. You probably think you deserve a pint, at this point, and it would be churlish to disagree so go on, treat yourself.

A hundred yards further up the road from the Grouse, take the footpath on the right, heading due E, then ESE on to open moorland. Practically at the top of the hill is the path which runs SW along White Edge, which is easy to follow. It takes you along White Edge for two miles, until you come to a cairn and the path forks. Fork right and you come out on to the road by the car park.

WALK 4: Robin Hood-Nelson's Monument-Wellington's Monument-Moorside Farm

Some outlaw or other is supposed to have been born in these parts – significantly, there is a suburb of Sheffield, some eight miles north of here, called Loxley – and the locals are very big on the connection. Take this place, for instance, on the A619 Chesterfield-Baslow road. The village is called Robin Hood, the pub is called the Robin Hood, and there is a farm called Robin Hood Farm. Wonder what the name of the outlaw was?

This is a little walk, though it covers some very dramatic and rough territory and has the supreme advantage of starting and finishing at a pub. Park in the car park 100 yds east of the pub, emerging from the car doing your best Errol Flynn impersonation. 'Welcome to Sherwood!' would be the thing to say, were Sherwood not 50 miles away.

Moderate going, two gentle climbs.
4½ miles, 2 hrs.
Start SK281721.

From the car park go on to the road and turn left. A hundred yards later take the footpath on the left, and make your way up Birchen Edge, past Nelson's Monument, to the trig point at the top of the hill. You can see Nelson and Wellington facing each other across the valley. Nelson was here first, erected by a local dignitary. Another local dignitary thought Wellington was not being well done by, so stuck up another bit of rock. Pause to consider whether it would have been better if both had simply left well alone.

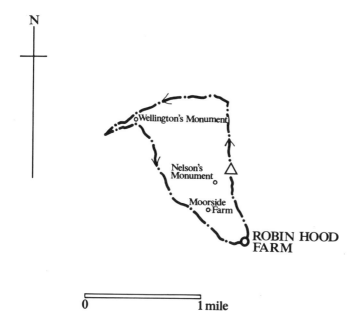

Wellington's Monument

Nelson's
Monument

Moorside
Farm

ROBIN HOOD
FARM

0   1 mile

From the trig point head due N-ish, to the crossroads where the Sheffield road and Curbar lane cross. There is a stile on the S side of the crossroads which brings you out on to the main road. Cross the road, face right and take the turning on the left, signposted to Curbar.

About 75 yds down this lane, take the well-defined footpath on the left, through a gate. This heads W a way and then turns SW across Eaglestone Flat (Wellington's Monument is now to your left).

When this path starts to come down steeply off the flat, take the footpath on the left, almost doubling back on yourself, which sticks to the left-hand side of a wall and heads into the woods beneath the Wellington Monument. Once into the woods, the path bends right and heads downhill to the main road in the valley bottom.

Cross the main road and take the footpath opposite to the left of the cottage. This bends right almost immediately, and climbs the other side of the valley underneath Gardom's Edge before entering the Moorside Farm Estate of the National Trust, with its stone-age enclosure.

You come out on to the A619. Turn left and you will find yourself back in Robin Hood.

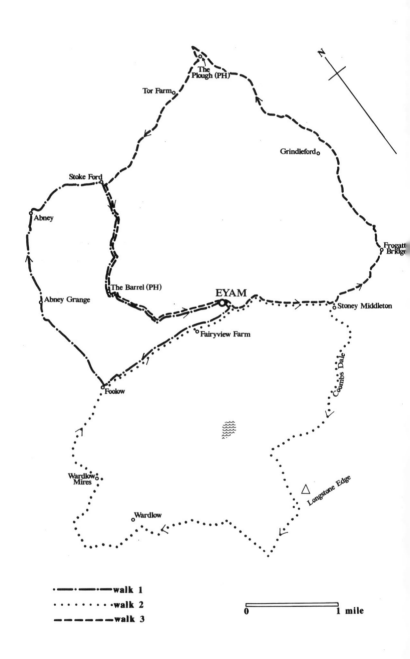

The Plough (PH)
Tor Farm
Grindleford
Stoke Ford
Abney
Frogatt Bridge
The Barrel (PH)
EYAM
Fairview Farm
Stoney Middleton
Abney Grange
Coombs Dale
Foolow
Longstone Edge
Wardlow Mires
Wardlow

N

•—•—•—•—• walk 1

•••••••••• walk 2

———————— walk 3

0   1 mile

EYAM

Eyam is famous for having endured the plague in the 17th century – the villagers cut themselves off from the outside world to avoid infecting others – and it now attracts a healthy living from this morbid past. There are commemorative plaques everywhere – and tourists reading them. But it remains a charming, if at times somewhat crowded place, and it's in the heart of some wonderful walking country.

There is a car park on Hawkhill Road – the minor road to Hathersage north from the main street.

WALK 1: Eyam-Foolow-Abney-Bretton

A reasonably short, but surprisingly arduous walk, though one which pays great dividends for those who appreciate a constantly changing vista (and the occasional good pub) with their walks.

Moderate going, steep climbing.
8 miles, 3½ hrs.
Start SK216767.

From the car park turn left on to the road and head downhill into the village proper. Turn left again on to the main street, and turn right, 250 yds later, past the Rose and Crown, into New Close.

At the end of this, climb up the steps on to the path between the modern houses. This heads due W uphill, across a couple of lanes and out of the village.

It's one-and-a-half miles to Foolow, and the path is easy to follow. It crosses the curious little Linen Dale and, shortly thereafter, forks at a barn and signpost. Fork right across one field to the road and turn left into Foolow.

Pass the Lazy Landlord on your right and take the road on the right, signposted to Bretton. After 500 yds the road starts to bend right. Take the signposted footpath on the left which continues the road's former line. This runs alongside a wall and heads dead straight up the steep hill in front of you, coming out on to the road which runs along the top.

Cross the road and take the footpath opposite, down the other side of the hill and over the head of Bretton Clough – making for the large farm you see on the other side.

The footpath emerges on to a metalled lane. Turn right and follow it past the front of the farm and on to the road, turning right once more. Follow this downhill and through some woods into Abney (a few houses, a B&B and a phone box, but very pretty). Take the footpath on the right signposted to Stoke Ford and Eyam. It descends to the bottom of Abney Clough and enters a wood, on the other side of which is Stoke Ford, the place where Abney Clough and Bretton Clough meet.

Take the footpath on the right (the one which climbs the least), keeping almost to the bottom of the clough running in that direction – Bretton Clough. The path does climb, but gently, and stays well within the confines of the clough (which is just as well as otherwise the headless horseman which haunts it wouldn't be able to get you).

After a few hundred yards it climbs a smaller clough to the right before resuming its former heading (roughly SW) and following the left side of a wall through the wood. This brings you out of the trees and on to a lane. Turn right and follow it gently uphill to Bretton. Time for a pint in the Barrel? There is nothing better on a summer's evening than sitting outside watching the view from the top of the edge here.

From the Barrel take the road left for 150 yds, taking the next signposted footpath on the right, which descends Eyam Edge diagonally (passing the rather unsightly Black Hole Mine) and joining the Foolow road. Turn left and follow it back to Eyam (three-quarters of a mile).

WALK 2: Eyam-Stoney Middleton-Wardlow-Foolow

A walk with constant reminders of the Peak's past, not least in Eyam itself. It goes past a working mine and some clearly visible 18th-century workings, drops in at three very different villages, and passes through two steep-sided dales and some wild moorland.

Moderate and easy going, substantial climbing.
11 miles, 4½ hours.
Start SK216767.

Make your way from the car park to the High Street and turn left, following it past the Rose and Crown, shops and the church. If there are not too many crowds about, it is interesting to read the plaques on the houses telling of how they were involved in the 17th-century plague, and just to admire a well-preserved and attractive village.

This brings you to the square. Opposite and to the left, take Lydgate (past the graves of a family of plague victims) and, at the end, join the footpath to Stoney Middleton. This goes gently downhill more or less SE for more or less a mile, coming out on Middleton's old main road, the Bank.

Turn right, down to the noisy A623, passing to the left of the octagonal tollbooth where a fee used to be exacted for passing through the village. Climb the steep metalled path opposite and to the left of the

Royal Oak, bringing you out on to another road. Turn right and shortly afterwards left down a narrow lane called Eaton Fold.

Keep left past the houses, and bend left into the next field before a barn. Here swing right and head downhill, making your way on to the metalled lane along the dale bottom. This is Coombs Dale. Turn right and follow the lane.

After a mile of pleasantly wooded dale the landscape becomes suddenly, and strangely, industrial as you enter the Sallet Hole Mine site. Pass the works buildings and you can see the entrance to the mine on your left as the dale bends right. Worry about the sign warning about the remote controlled vehicles in use.

Carry on for another three-quarters of a mile, until you approach the dale head – there is a high bank in front of you. When you come to a signpost, with paths to Foolow, Wardlow and Longstone Edge indicated, turn left (along the footpath to Longstone Edge) and climb the dale side.

This is a long and sometimes muddy climb. It brings you to a lane leading to the fluorspar workings on High Rake. Turn right for 25 yds to a minor road, then turn left and follow the road around a right-hand bend and look at the view to your left.

Here there is a vivid illustration of how radically different the geography within the Peak District can be. You can see the gritstone edges above Baslow and Froggat to the east, and to the south are some of the Peak's great dales – Monsal Dale is slightly over to the right.

Cross a cattle-grid and enter a wood, following the road around a left bend until you come to a footpath sign pointing uphill NNW. Take this footpath to the right and climb through the wood and on to Longstone Moor. This is a beautiful spot at any time of the year, but perhaps best in spring when the wild flowers are blooming, and in a dry autumn when you can sometimes get strange colour combinations – for example a blue sky with yellowing vegetation and purple heather.

Just after the signpost at the highest point of the moor (about 250 yds further on) there is a rake (a natural mineralised fault) running across the hillside. Turn left and follow this diagonally downhill to a road.

Cross the road and take the footpath opposite, noting the well-preserved mine workings on your left as you enter the field. This path takes you WNW to the road S of Wardlow.

Turn right on the road. Follow it for 200 yds, then take the lane to the left, signposted as the footpath to Ravensdale.* At the end of the lane the footpath forks. Go right and make your way down into the dale, a superb rocky, steep-sided one, and follow the bottom N.

*If tired, you can save yourself a climb (though you miss a great bit of the walk out) by taking the road straight to Wardlow Mires.

As you climb to the head of the dale, it bends right and ends up heading ENE, coming out on to the A623 at Wardlow Mires. Turn right on the road, passing the junction and the Three Stags' Heads. Opposite the garage, turn left between the globe-topped gateposts of a farm, and follow the footpath left through the farmyard. Then follow it NNW uphill across fields to a stile on to a lane and turn right past a farmhouse.

The lane starts to bend right. Just after a turning-off to the left, cross the stile and take the footpath on the left diagonally across two fields, crossing the lane again and proceeding across more fields to emerge on the village green at Foolow.

Turn right on to the main road. Time, perhaps, to drop in for a pint at the Lazy Landlord, if you are not discouraged by the landlord's sign forbidding wet or muddy boots and clothing (not that the carpets inside are particularly spectacular).

Past the Landlord, carry straight on at the junction on the edge of the village, along the Eyam road. Just past the Foolow boundary sign, take the footpath on the right, bending left at a ramshackle barn across the first field. This footpath heads E and brings you out, one-and-a-half miles later, by the Rose and Crown in Eyam. Turning left then right will take you back to the car park.

WALK 3: Eyam-Froggat-Leadmill-Bretton

A walk designed with variety in mind, it explores upland pasture, riverside fields, woods and moorland.

Easy and moderate going, one long climb.
11 miles, 4 hrs.
Start SK216767.

Follow Walk 2 to Stoney Middleton and turn left on coming out on to the old main road. Follow this round a right-hand bend, past the cottages, taking the turning on the left to the church. Follow this left round the churchyard, then right, having a look at the old bath-house (which is now being restored by the National Park). There is a thermal spring here, with water emerging from below ground at a constant 67 degrees Celsius.

Shortly after this, where the lane bends left, carry straight on through the kissing gate. Follow the well-worn path E, forking left at the next stile, which will take you through the farmyard of Knouchley Farm and on to the Grindleford-Calver road. Cross over and take the footpath opposite, bending left after the first field to go down to the riverside path.

Turn right on the next road, crossing the bridge into Froggat. Turn left on the other side and follow this road for 150 yds until it bends right by the Methodist chapel. Take the lane (signposted as a footpath) which carries straight on. This climbs very gently, becoming a distinct footpath when it starts to descend into some woods. It brings you out, after a mile, in Nether Padley.

Turn right on the road, taking the footpath on the left 75 yds later. This runs parallel to the river across three fields before forking. Go left to the riverbank and follow it for a mile-and-a-half, diverging slightly only to cut out a bend in the river after passing through a wood.

The river then takes a serious left bend, and the path follows it, to emerge on to the road. Turn left and cross the river, following the road past the Plough Inn and the road to Abney, taking the next turning on the right, to Hazelford and Leam.

The road climbs quite steeply, passing a couple of houses before bending right and then bending crazily left, uphill, into some trees. At this point, take the farm lane on the right which carries on the line of the road, into a valley.

Pass the farm and follow the path W and SW for a mile-and-a-quarter, into then out of a wood, to Stoke Ford where three cloughs and five paths meet.

Turn left and follow the footpath to Bretton. It heads SSW, climbing only very gently out of the bottom of Bretton Clough. After a few hundred yards it climbs a smaller clough to the right before resuming its former heading (roughly SW) and following the left side of a wall through the wood. This brings you out of the trees and on to a lane. Turn right and follow it gently uphill to Bretton and the Barrel (see Walk 1).

From the Barrel take the road on the left for 150 yds, taking the next signposted footpath on the right, which descends Eyam Edge diagonally (passing the rather unsightly Black Hole Mine) and joining the Foolow road. Turn left and follow it back to Eyam (three-quarters of a mile).

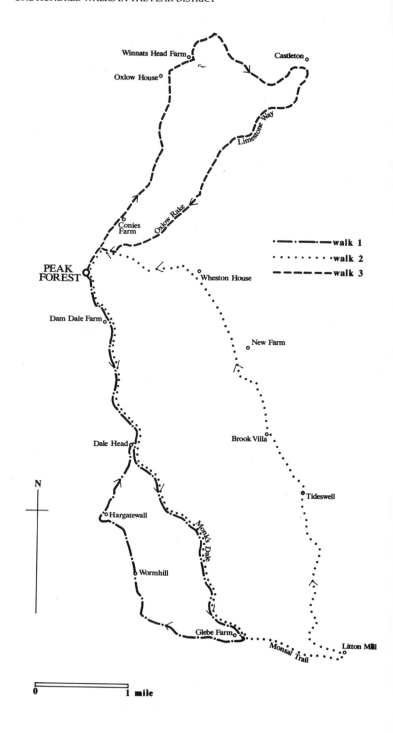

PEAK FOREST

Peak Forest is one of the those Peak District forests (like Hope Forest to the north-east) without trees – the name refers to a hunting range or game reserve. The village has an interesting history: the church was, in the 17th and 18th centuries, free from Church of England central jurisdiction, and became one of those places people eloped to as they could get married here at short notice (and for a fee). Also, on the hill north of the village, there is a natural vertical cave called Eldon Hole. This was long thought to be bottomless, the gateway to Hell, that sort of thing. From late medieval to relatively modern times people tried to measure its depth, paying in two miles of rope without reaching the bottom and, at one point, lowering a man down only to have him expire without saying a word on his return to the surface. It's 180 feet deep.

WALK 1: Peak Forest-Dam Dale-Miller's Dale-Wormhill-Dam Dale

A walk down the long gorge which runs south from Peak Forest to the River Wye, climbing up on to the limestone top before plunging back down into the long dale again. Part of the string of dales is a nature reserve, and all of it is magnificent to look at.

Easy-moderate going, one climb.
10 miles, 3½ hrs.
Start SK113794.

Opposite the pub, follow Damside Lane S, past a farm. At the end of the lane, turn left, then quickly right over a stile, into a long field. Make for the corner diagonally opposite (and another farm).

Past the farmyard the way down into Dam Dale is clear – carry straight on and the dale closes in around you. The dale changes its name three times before its end – it will become Hay Dale at its first bend, then Peter Dale and finally Monk's Dale. Do you want to know about the werewolf which is supposed to haunt this area? No, probably not.

Follow the dale until you can follow it no further, climbing the left side of the head of Monk's Dale to emerge beside the church of the tiny hamlet of Miller's Dale.

Opposite is a turning off the main road. Go down it and, a little way along it, take the footpath on the right over the river (unless you fancy a pint in the Angler's Rest, a little further along the road).

This climbs the opposite bank of the river, emerging, through some woods, on to an old railway track. This is the Monsal Trail. Turn right and follow it W back over the river (over the impressive viaduct you will have noticed from beside the church) and through the old Miller's Dale Station.

The trail then bends right, to the NW, then back to the W. About 250 yds after this, take the footpath on the right which climbs uphill diagonally, soon turning N to climb steeply up a very short dale and emerge across a field and on to the road at Wormhill.

Turn left on the road, bending right, and follow it through the village until you come, almost three-quarters of a mile later, to a crossroads. Go straight over, into the hamlet of Hargatewall. As the road bends left you will pass Hargate Hall on your right, pass two lanes off to your right and then come to a farm entrance (Hayward Farm) with a footpath sign. Take this to the right and follow the lane it gives on to roughly NE over fields for almost half a mile.

As it nears the lip of Peter Dale, the path turns N, then descends sharply (and muddily) to the road. Turn right and, 100 yds later, left back on to the path along the Dale bottom. Retrace your steps back to Peak Forest.

WALK 2: Peak Forest-Dam Dale-Miller's Dale-Tideswell-Old Dam

A gentle walk exploring the dales and ending with a burst of limestone moor. It is reasonably long, but gentle, and goes through some quite delightful scenery.

Easy and moderate going, one gentle climb.
12 miles, 5 hrs.
Start SK113794.

Follow Walk 1 as far as the Monsal Trail, and turn left. (If you've been for a pint in the Angler's or simply don't fancy climbing the opposite bank of Miller's Dale, carry on along the lane, and we'll catch you up later.)

Follow the trail for a mile E, until it descends to the left (the tunnel ahead being unsafe), over the river and into Litton Mill. Turn left on the road, past the tea shop.

After 400 yds there's an impressive rock face on your right. Take the signposted footpath on the right immediately after this, at a lay-by into Tideswell Dale. (Ah, here you are, you waited for us.) If you find yourself climbing at this point, you're on the wrong path and heading for the Youth Hostel – the one you wanted was further to the right.

Three-quarters of a mile of winding, wooded path through Tideswell Dale brings you, through a car park and picnic area, on to a road. Turn right two hundred yards later, cross the road and take the footpath on the left immediately to the right of the water treatment plant (i.e. sewage farm). This climbs a little then turns right and heads parallel to the road. Emerging on to a minor road, take the lane opposite down into the village proper. This brings you out past the Horse and Jockey, a fine pub.

Follow the main street N, until it forks, taking the fork on the left (though it is worth going right and having a look at the church, the 'cathedral of the Peak'), which will bring you into the market place. Opposite the Star, and by the Oddfellow's Hall, take the road off to the left, and follow it NW for a mile, out of the village and into a small dale called Brook Bottom.

It will bring you on to the busy A623. Go left for 300 yds, until a stile on the right, crossing which, take the footpath NW (i.e. diagonally left across the field). After several (alright, three) fields, you cross a lane and carry on in more or less the same direction, bending slightly left after the third field, crossing another lane by a long farmhouse and coming into a field with a pond in the far right-hand corner. The next field has a millstone set on edge in it.

Here take the footpath on the left, bringing you on to a lane with another lane opposite. Take the lane opposite and follow it for half a mile, until you come to a crossroads. The road back to Peak Forest (400 yds away) is on the left.

WALK 3: Peak Forest-Winnat's-Castleton-Cavedale

A walk over limestone tops to some of the most attractive (and popular) scenery in the Peak.

Moderate going, one climb.
8½ miles, 3½ hrs.
Start SK113794.

Take the road out of Peak Forest to Old Dam. At the end (a T-junction) take the lane opposite, to the right of the row of cottages. This climbs, NNW, to the left of a farm then swings NW for a mile, on to the moor.

The lane comes to a place where five ways meet. Cross the walled lane and take the footpath going diagonally left, on the right side of a wall running NNE. Once over the brow of the hill you have a glorious uninterrupted view across fields to Mam Tor, with its distinctive broken east face, and Winnat's, where the only road into Castleton from the west plunges down into a deep defile.

Head straight for Mam Tor, coming out at a road. Turn right to a corner, and carry straight on down the road signposted to Castleton (light traffic only).

Immediately after the farm on the left and the gate, take the signposted footpath on the left. This goes past the entrance to the Blue

John Cavern, swinging around the hillside to the E, and starts to descend steeply along Treak Cliff, parallel to what used to be the main road until it disappeared in a landslide in the early 70s.

Cross the road at the bottom of Winnat's Pass, to the left of the Speedwell Cavern, and follow the contours of the hill around into Castleton, coming out on a lane which leads into the village. You will be able to see the imposing entrance to Peak Cavern to your right. Cross the stream and go down the narrow lane past the chip shop into the Market Place.

Unless you fancy a pint in the George (to the left), cross the Market Place with its small shops on the right-hand side, and turn right up the signposted entrance to Cave Dale, just after Bargate Cottage (painted an 'interesting' shade of blue).

Go through the gate and climb the dale. At its head you will come to a crossroads, with five ways meeting at a signpost. Cross the stile opposite into the pointy corner of a field and take the footpath running alongside the wall to the left.*

This takes you up on to Bradwell Moor, a glorious bit of wild land with magnificent views to the north and north-east. After almost a mile, you will be able to see a gate in front of you and some open-cast mine workings running down the hill.

Take the footpath on the right over the stile and descend WSW. This follows a worked-out rake (a mineralised geological fault) part of the way, then crosses pasture, to come to a meeting of ways. Take the lane opposite, follow it to a crossroads, and turn back into Peak Forest.

*It is quicker at this point (by half a mile) to take the path by the wall on the right, signposted to Peak Forest. But it is less interesting.

Old Dam (Peak Forest)

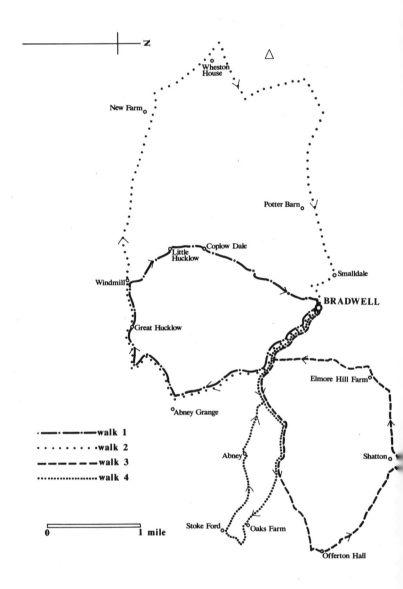

Wheston House

New Farm

Potter Barn

Coplow Dale

Little Hucklow

Windmill

Smalldale

BRADWELL

Great Hucklow

Elmore Hill Farm

Abney Grange

Abney

Shatton

Stoke Ford

Oaks Farm

Offerton Hall

·—·—·—·—walk 1
············walk 2
— — — — walk 3
···············walk 4

0   1 mile

BRADWELL

A charming and out-of-the-way village on the road between the Hope Valley and Tideswell. It's called 'Bradda' by the locals, for some unknown reason. The hills around here are limestone, and because their natural beauty is somewhat disrupted in places by industrial development – the huge cement factory and various open-cast mining sites – and there are relatively few walkers. Nevertheless, there is a lot of good walking to be had.

WALK 1: Bradwell-Abney Moor-the Hucklows-Green Dale

A walk over varied limestone countryside: Abney Moor can be beautifully tranquil, and the two Hucklow villages, Great and Little, are both charming (and both have excellent pubs).

Moderate going with one steep climb.
7 miles, 2½ hrs.
Start SK174812.

Starting at the S end of the village green and facing S on the main street (opposite the Valley Lodge pub) climb the little flight of steps leading off to the left. At the top, turn left then turn into Bessie Lane. Follow this downhill and round to the right for 400 yds, past some new houses, and then left, uphill.

This brings you to a stile giving on to a footpath which winds its way uphill through some hawthorn scrub. Where this path forks at the remains of an old stone stile, take the path on the right, which leads up to Robin Hood's Cross (there are all sorts of references to Robin Hood in the place names of the district, but this is one of the oldest and, therefore, most likely to be genuine).

Following the path all the way up to the top of the hill you will come to a lane. Turn right and go through the gate. A little further on there is a footpath on the right, signposted to Great Hucklow, which you should take and which leads you on to Abney Moor proper. In the summer sunshine and with the skylarks singing this is a glorious spot.

On the other side of the moor you emerge on to a road. Turn right and take the footpath on the left just after a lane. This takes you down over the head of Bretton Clough, past the gliding club and brings you out on to the road you just left by a pumping station. Turn left and follow the road as it bends left into some woods.

You pass a lane off to the right, and then some railings, immediately after which is the overgrown footpath on the right which leads downhill into Great Hucklow. At the bottom, turn right and walk into the village. Is the Queen Anne open? Do you fancy a pint? Do you resent the sign in the window that tells you to take your muddy boots off? It's entirely up to you.

Heading W out of Great Hucklow on the road, you come half a mile later to a crossroads. Cross the main road, taking the lane opposite into the hamlet of Windmill where there is an inn, according to the OS map. See if you can find it (I very much doubt it as it appears not to exist).

Take the footpath to the right immediately to the right of Cherry Tree Cottage. This leads you up and down over the undulating limestone NW to Little Hucklow (which you can see from Windmill). Once there turn left on the road, past the Bull's Head and repeat the Queen Anne dilemma, except that there is no muddy-boots sign here.

The road bends right then left past the pub, and 50 yds further on take the signposted footpath on the right, which leads more or less due N to Coplow Dale. (Cop Low itself is a neolithic burial mound 300 yds up the road to the right.) Here take the footpath opposite and to the right.

This, again, goes up and down, leading away NE over several fields and emerging on to a minor road at the head of Green Dale. The most interesting way back to Bradwell from here is probably to turn left on the road and follow it – this does mean you can call in at the Bagshawe Cavern as you get back, if you're up for a spot of dilettante speleology. On the other hand, you could take the lane down Green Dale, and turn left at the bottom, following the main road back into the village, which gets you a look at the attractive Bradwell Dale (though the road spoils it a bit).

WALK 2: Bradwell-Abney Moor-Great Hucklow-Tideslow-Bradwell

Similar in character to Walk 1, except that this walk goes on to explore a couple of the local rakes – geological faults running straight across country – and the wild Bradwell Moor.

Moderate going with one steep climb.
11 miles, 4 hrs.
Start SK174812.

Follow Walk 1 as far as Windmill. Instead of turning right here, carry straight on along the road out of the hamlet. After a few hundred yards the road bends left, then right, then left again. To your left is the start of High Rake (a knobbly geographical feature).

Take the path off to the left along the rake. It is not signposted as such, though there is a sign to Castleton Lane further on. Because the rake is so knobbly, it has been left pretty much undisturbed by generations of farmers, and so is a great place for wild flowers in spring, and for birds and butterflies according to the season.

High Rake goes on for about 500 yds, until it meets Castleton Lane. Cross this road and continue along Tideslow Rake, which you can see climbing up the hillside – it looks as though some giant, in an idle moment, has gouged a line in the land with a very large stick – but it does mean that it's very hard to lose your way.

Follow the rake over Tides Low, where there is a neolithic burial mound and a more recent radio mast, and head down the other side of the hill. The path does occasionally close because of the open-cast fluorspar workings, but there is always an alternative footpath provided.

This brings you out on to a minor road, and the continuing footpath is opposite and to the right. This brings you to another road. Turn left and walk for 200 yds, taking the next footpath on the right, which heads across Tideswell Moor parallel to the main A623 road (you can see it from time to time).

After half a mile across fields, you cross a lane by a long, low farmhouse. At the end of the next field there is a natural spring called Adam's Well on your right, and in the next field there is a millstone set on its edge. Turn right here and head slightly back on yourself (roughly ENE) without heading too far uphill.

This takes you up a small valley to the start of a rake, which you follow uphill to the track which runs across Bradwell Moor. There used, here, to be a path which went down the other side of this hill – down Moss Rake and straight into Bradwell – but the rake has now been destroyed by mineral workings, so it is now better to turn left here, and head over the moor for three-quarters of a mile, taking the footpath on the right when you come downhill from the moor and come to a gate. This path heads NE for two fields before turning SE and descending to Castleton Lane.

When you emerge on the lane, take the lane opposite, signposted to Smalldale. Turning right 500 yds later, when you are amongst the houses of Smalldale, will bring you back to Bradwell.

WALK 3: Bradwell-Abney Moor-Shatton Moor

A pleasant walk on a beautiful hill on the unfashionable, neglected south side of the Hope Valley, offering fantastic panoramas as well as interesting immediate surroundings. This walk takes you by Rebellion Knoll and the Reform Stone, place names which testify to unrest amongst the lead-miners who used to work these hills at the time of the French Revolution.

Mainly easy going with two climbs.
7½ miles, 3 hrs.
Start SK174812.

Follow Walk 1 to Robin Hood's Cross, turning right on to the lane but staying on it rather than taking the footpath. The lane bends left, over the next half mile, through 180 degrees. At the most severe left bend, take the footpath on the right.

This will take you E along the edge of the moor before turning SE and descending. You pass a broad track off to the left, and then, 100 yds further on, take the footpath on the left, climbing slightly to the right of a cairn.

This path heads over a spur of the hill and then begins its descent towards Offerton Hall. The Reform Stone stands on the brow of the hill to your right, about half a mile further on, just before you begin to descend steeply.

You come, eventually, to a lane. Turn left and follow it downhill, past Offerton Hall and various other buildings. Where it forks, 400 yds later, fork left, heading NW towards the distinctive bulk of Win Hill on the other side of the valley.

Stick to the lane and, a mile later, you will find yourself in Shatton, an unfortunately named, but not unattractive, hamlet. Turn left at the end of the lane, then first right, heading due W along Townfield Lane.

Five hundred yards later, pass a turning off to the left, then, after another 250 yds, fork left once again, heading uphill to the right of the farm in front of you.

This will bring you to a T-junction with another lane. Turn left* and climb uphill. As you climb and look down to your right, you will be able to see a straight mound running up the hill. This is the Grey Ditch – the remains of a bronze-age defensive earthwork. You will also pass over Rebellion Knoll. The lane then brings you back to Robin Hood's Cross, at which point turn right and head back down into Bradwell.

*If knackered at this point, take the footpath opposite, which does not do any more climbing and heads over the Grey Ditch and straight into Bradwell.

WALK 4: Bradwell-Smelting Hill-Abney

A pretty little walk through moorland and woods, perfect for a summer evening.

Moderate going (harder in wet weather) with two climbs.
5½ miles, 2½ hrs.
Start SK174812.

Follow Walk 1 to Robin Hood's Cross. Instead of turning right off the lane at the top of the hill, follow it as it bends left, first E and then NE.

At a place called Wolf's Pit, the lane takes a very tight bend around to the left, and there is a footpath on the right a little further on, which takes you along the edge of Abney Moor, heading due E. Five hundred yards further on, on Smelting Hill (the place names Wolf's Pit, Smelting Hill and so on are redolent of the area's lead-mining past) it starts to turn to the SE, and descends to a farm.

Head to the right of the farm and turn left on a path running to the right of the woods to the E. This path soon bends right and heads downhill to the road into Abney.

Cross over the road and take the footpath opposite, downhill, to the bottom of Abney Clough. Pretty, isn't it? Just before you get to the stream, take the well-defined path on the right running along the bottom of the clough through the woods. Perhaps now is the time, especially if it is latish in the evening and there is a hint of twilight down here, to reflect on the fact that this area is the haunt of one of the Peak District's many ghosts – a headless horseman. Then again, perhaps not.

There is just less than a mile of the clough before it turns NW and you climb sharply into the tiny village of Abney. Turn left on the village street, and then, 150 yds later, before the phone box, take the lane right, which climbs back up on to the moor and brings you back on to the moor lane. Turn left at the top and it will bring you back to Robin Hood's Cross and, thence, to Bradwell.

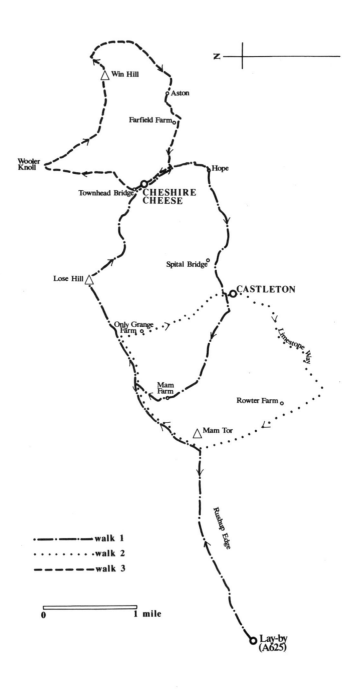

CASTLETON

Amongst the biggest tourist draws in the Peak District, Castleton is often crowded with people wandering around its streets, poking about in its tourist attractions (especially the caves and the castle) and buying blue john, the mineral mined locally and nowhere else. It has some fine pubs (try the George) and is at the end of the 272 bus route from Sheffield. You can also get there by taking the train to Hope and walking two miles west from the station.

WALK 1: Rushup-Mam Tor-Lose Hill-Hope-Castleton-Mam Tor

An easy but rewarding ridgewalk followed by a delightful lowland ramble and a stiff climb back to the beginning. There's also a great pub at the halfway point. This walk starts from the A625 three-and-a-half miles W of Castleton – there is a substantial lay-by for parking just W of the footpath, and very close to the turning S for Perryfoot.

Moderate going, one hard climb.
13 miles, 5 hrs.
Start SK093825.

From the lay-by on the N side of the road, head E. Take the first footpath on the left – it runs along the left side of the wall and is in a curious dip or rut. Follow this path along Rushup Edge for two miles, dipping down on to the road and climbing the footpath opposite to the top of Mam Tor (the 'shivering mountain', so called because it's made of shales and clay which trap a lot of water, though the quantity varies according to the prevailing conditions, so the hill contracts or expands accordingly).

Continue along the ridge for another two miles, until it finishes. This involves some climbing, especially as you climb Lose Hill (pronounced 'loose hill'), the steep little pimple at the very end. The view from here, however, is terrific.

From the cairn on top of Lose Hill, turn right and take the footpath running straight downhill. After you have crossed a stone wall, look for and take the path which bears left slightly, to take you ESE. This leads down to Hope Townhead. As the descent is easing off it joins a farm lane. Keep heading in more or less the same direction and you will come out on to a bend in Edale Road.

Turn right on to the road. On your right you will pass the Cheshire Cheese, arguably the finest pub in this part of Derbyshire. It would be a shame not to venture inside.

Having slaked your thirst, or not, continue down the road to the T-junction with the major road opposite the church. Turn right and take the first road on the left, Pindale Road, though an amusing (some people find it shocking) diversion is to enter the churchyard and examine the gargoyles to see if you can find the extremely rude one (it is auto-fellatative).

Pass the first turning left, and then, where the road forks, go right (passing on your right the pinfold, where straying livestock were kept to be released on payment of a fine). Shortly after, take the footpath on the right, signposted to Castleton. Particularly in its later sections where it follows the Peakshole Water, this is a charming walk, and a good one for the wild flower enthusiast.

This brings you to the main road. Turn left and enter Castleton, following the road round a left and right bend, passing the Peak, then bending left and right again, past the Nag's Head. Once past the castle, the garage and all the houses on the left, take the footpath on the right to a stream, and follow this WNW until it comes to a meeting of ways.

You have a choice of paths here, the object being to get to the top of the hill as comfortably as possible. Ignore the farm lane running left and right. The footpath opposite which carries straight on allows you to climb the hill relatively gently, but is longer than the footpath opposite and right, which heads straight for Hollins Cross. Once there, however, there is only one way back – turn left and retrace your steps along the ridge, over Mam Tor and Rushup.

WALK 2: Castleton-Cavedale-Mam Tor-Back Tor

This walk climbs a delightful limestone dale at the back of the village, on to limestone moors and along the Mam Tor ridge before descending back to the village. On summer weekends and in the peak season it is not a walk for those seeking isolation and serenity, as it can get rather crowded in places. It starts from the car park on Castleton's main road.

Moderate going, one long climb.
6½ miles, 2½ hrs.
Start SK149829.

From the car park return to the main road and turn left, turning right by the Castle Hotel into Church Street. Follow this past the George and into the Market Place, turning left at the bottom into Bargate.

After Bargate Cottage (an alarming shade of blue), take the footpath on the right (signposted) and enter Cavedale. Climb the path along the bottom of the dale (over a mile) until you emerge on the limestone plateau.

Coming to a meeting of ways (there's a signpost), take the walled farm lane on the right, following it round to the right 200 yds later. This takes you past a farm and, almost a mile later, on to the road by Windy Knoll.

Cross the road and take the footpath opposite, which will bring you to another road after 400 yds. Cross this on to the footpath opposite, which takes you uphill to a third road. Here, turn right and climb the footpath to the top of Mam Tor.

Having surveyed the view and got your breath back, carry on along the ridge for a mile and a half. The path will narrow somewhat, and you will come to Back Tor Nook, a curious dip in the ridge before a steep climb to a cliff on the left side of the hill.

In this dip turn right and follow the path diagonally downhill. Turning left when you come to a low stone wall and follow right around its protruding corner, making your way to the right of the farm which lies directly downhill.

Continue, over stiles, in the same direction, joining a track which brings you, half a mile later after the farm, to a lane. Turn right then, 150 yds later, left, and you are now on the lane which will bring you out on to a corner of the main street in Castleton.

To get back to the car park, carry straight on and turn right at the Nag's Head.

WALK 3: Hope-Win Hill-Aston

This is a hill walk in the traditional sense – i.e. it's a walk up a hill and back down again. It's quite short, but it does cover an astonishing variety of types of ground: wooded lowlands, pasture, open moorland, plantation and farmland.

It starts and finishes at the Cheshire Cheese on Edale Road in Hope. To get there from Castleton, take the A625 E, turning left opposite Hope Church. The Cheese is half a mile down the road. Parking is limited here – an alternative car park can be found on Castleton Road.

Moderate going, one long climb.
5 miles, 2 hrs.
Start SK170841.

Standing with your back to the Cheese, turn left and walk up Edale Road. Presently, you will come to a turning off to the left signposted as a dead-end, after which the road bends right. Follow it a little way further as it crosses the River Noe, taking the lane which carries straight on (there are footpaths and access signs) where the road bends left.

This lane crosses over the railway and starts to climb, turning left at a farm and climbing more steeply, but very prettily, on to the open moorside.

When you are in open pasture, the path forks. Head slightly right, uphill. At the crest of the shoulder of the hill, turn right again, taking the broad path which you can see climbing the shoulder.

Follow this as it bends left and climbs to the very top of Win Hill Pike, the rocky little outcrop at the end. Time for a spot of viewing. You can speculate on what this view used to look like before the reservoirs were here (nicer, is my guess), but also reflect that this is the scene of one of the greatest of all post-war British cinematic triumphs, indeed, one of the Great Moments in Cinema History – some of the action sequences for the Dambusters were filmed on the Ladybower and Derwent Reservoirs. (Come to think of it, that wasn't such a good film after all. Quite poor, in fact.)

Take the footpath down the other side of Win Hill Pike, passing through a gate stile when you come to a stone wall, and heading down into the plantation. Here you need to turn right at the first opportunity, keeping your height and following the left side of a wall for 400 yds before striking off right (uphill for a little way) and making your way, across fields, downhill to Aston.

This will bring you on to a minor road by some houses. Turn right and follow the road through the village (though, in truth, Aston is little more than a very loose string of houses), past a left turn and around a long, sweeping left bend.

After half a mile of road, take the footpath on the right along the lane to Farfield Farm. The lane passes the farm, then crosses underneath the railway before joining another lane by some pretty cottages in Hope. Turn left and cross the river to the road, turning right on the road for the Cheese (or left for Hope village if you parked on Castleton Road and don't fancy a pint).

Mam Tor from Hollins Cross (Castleton)

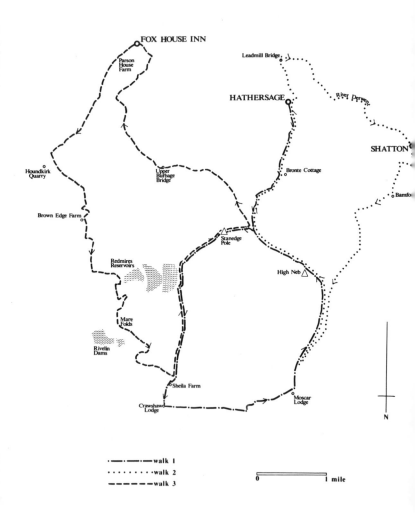

FOX HOUSE INN

Parson House Farm

Leadmill Bridge

River Derwent

HATHERSAGE

SHATTON

Houndkirk Quarry

Upper Burbage Bridge

Bronte Cottage

Bamfo

Brown Edge Farm

Stanedge Pole

Redmires Reservoirs

High Neb

Mare Folds

Rivelin Dams

Sheila Farm

Crawshaw Lodge

Moscar Lodge

N

·—·—·—walk 1
· · · · · ·walk 2
— — — —walk 3

0   1 mile

THE NORTH-EAST

HATHERSAGE

Hathersage is, to all intents and purposes, a suburb of Sheffield. It has a bank, a few pubs, a good outdoor shop, Little John's grave and a railway station. Other than that there is very little to it, except that it's surrounded by spectacular scenery – Stanage Edge, which must be one of the most popular climbing areas in the country, dominates the northern skyline.

The first two of these walks starts from the village – there is a clearly signposted car park off the Bakewell road. Walk 3 starts from the Fox House Inn on the Sheffield road (lots of buses stop right outside) for which drivers can use the Longshaw car park on the B6055.

WALK 1: Hathersage-Hallam Moors-Hollow Meadows-Stanage Edge

A long ascent on to the moors is followed by a tour of changing scenery and a dramatic return along the high edge with superb views to the west.

Moderate going, one hard climb and two gentler ascents.
12 miles, 5 hrs.
Start SK232813.

Take the footpath from the top of the car park on to the High Street, past the Methodist chapel. Take the lane opposite and to the right, which leads away from the village, slightly W of N beside a small tributary of the Derwent. After a few hundred yards, now a well-defined track, it bends right and starts to climb gently and, a mile from the village, meets a road.

Turn left then take the farm track immediately on the right. Keeping to the right of the farm, follow this to another road, coming out beside the mountain rescue post. Turn left and, again, take the next footpath on the right, up to the top of Stanage Edge, where a bit of a sit down and an admire of the view is in order. Most of the climbing is out of the way, now.

You should be able to see a broad, well-defined path heading a few degrees N of E, gently uphill, to Stanedge Pole, which marks the boundary between Yorkshire and Derbyshire. Once there, take the broad track leading downhill and NE, to the right of the plantation.

This brings you on to a lane running due N between the plantation and a reservoir. Follow it for a quarter of a mile, until it bends NE then, 100 yds later, take the footpath (signposted) leading due N. This climbs for a short way then begins a long, gentle descent into the Rivelin Valley. This is the time to reflect on the fact that you're only five miles from the centre of Sheffield but this is great countryside. It's a shame all of Sheffield isn't like this.

The path brings you, well over a mile later, to the A57 Manchester road. Cross it, and take the footpath opposite, climbing the other side of the valley to a minor road.

Turn left and follow the road for a mile, until it bends left and you rejoin the main road. It would, in a country with more sensible attitudes to access to the land, be possible here to carry on across the moor on the private track to Moscar, but since this bears signs saying Private, Keep Out, we have to conclude that the landowner is not of a liberal disposition.

On the main road turn right (at least there is a footpath). Carry on along here for half a mile, taking the footpath on the left back on to the moor just after the Derbyshire boundary. Follow this S, climbing, on to Stanage Edge, and then follow the path along the top of the edge for two-and-a-half miles to the place where you first joined it, underneath Stanedge Pole – you'll be able to see the minor road running parallel to the edge beneath you to your right. Turn right and retrace your steps into Hathersage.

WALK 2: Hathersage-Shatton-Bamford-Moscar

After a gentle, pastoral start, this walk climbs on to the high moor and returns to the start by way of the ridge-walk along Stanage Edge.

Easy and moderate going, one long climb.
12 miles, 5 hrs.
Start SK232813.

Turn right from the car park on to the road, then left on to the Grindleford/Bakewell road. Follow this out of the village and past the railway station, under the railway bridge and past the David Mellor Cutlery Factory (one of the nicest-looking factories you'll ever see. No idea what the cutlery's like though) which is worth a look at.

Over the Derwent Bridge (before the Plough Inn) take the footpath immediately to the right, running westwards by the side of the river for two-and-a-half miles. This can be a really pleasant riverside stroll in its own right, especially in the evening (if you don't mind midges).

It comes out on a lane in the hamlet of Shatton. (The locals get annoyed if you pronounce its name with equal emphasis on both syllables – wonder why?) Turn right and cross the river, emerging on the main road opposite the Garden and Pet Centre. Take the footpath just to the left of it, leading under the railway.

Having passed under the bridge, the path soon meets a lane. Turn right on this and follow it E into Bamford. You emerge (having crossed the river) on to a main road. Turn left and follow it uphill past the church and the Derwent Hotel.

Turn right up a lane called Fidler's Well (only one 'd' – the council erected a sign with two several years ago, but the residents whited the second one out). Over a crossroads, this becomes Bamford Clough. Follow it uphill until it peters out at the entrance to Clough House. To the right of the driveway, continue on up the overgrown lane. It climbs steeply uphill and comes out on the road at the edge of Bamford Moor. Turn right and, still climbing, take the next footpath on the left, which is signposted.

This heads due N and climbs just to the right of the top of the hill in front of you. Once there you can turn around and see where you've been and how high you've climbed and perhaps even, you deserve it, feel a little smug.

Make your way NE down on to the shoulder between your hill and the high edge (Stanage Edge) to your right. It can get a touch boggy here. The object of the next exercise is to follow the edge northwards until you can find a place to climb up on to it – the easiest place is at Stanage End, where the rocky cliff finishes and the ridge falls away.

Climb here and turn back on yourself, following the path along the top of the edge for two-and-a-half miles, first S, then SE. At the point where the second of two well-worn paths peel off to the left, take the path downhill to the right, past a plantation, emerging through a car park on to a road.

Turn left and follow the road to the mountain rescue post on your right. Here take the (signposted) footpath on your right, to the left of the building, and follow it straight downhill, keeping the woods on your left, past a farm, to another road.

Turn left here, and take the footpath immediately on the right, which is a broad track and leads downhill into Hathersage (1 mile).

WALK 3: Fox House-Burbage Moor-Hallam Moor-Burbage Rocks

A long but fairly easy walk over rough and spectacular country.

Easy and moderate going, gentle climbing.
14 miles, 6 hrs.
Start SK266803.

Facing Fox House Inn, turn right and follow the main road for 400 yds until it bends right. Here, follow the lane which carries on the line of the road NE on to the moor. It bends left, passing in front of a farm and carries on over the moor for almost two miles before coming to a plantation.

Just before the plantation, take the track on the left, which follows the line of the trees up to a road. Cross this and take the footpath opposite, leading N (though it sidesteps to avoid an old quarry) past a farm and on to a track. The track emerges through some gates on to Fulwood Lane.

Turn left and follow the lane around a right-hand bend and, after another half a mile, take the second footpath on the left, which leads along a farm track and then bends right and heads downhill to come out on another lane leading to a right-angled bend in the road.

On the road turn left, then left again down a road signposted as a dead end. Over a bridge, enter the Yorkshire Water car park on the right.* At the top right corner of this is a lane. At the corner where this joins the car park, take the signposted (but not very well) footpath on the left which climbs some steps and then bends right to follow the W perimeter of the woods.

The path bends NW after a while and, after heading this way for half a mile, bends right and heads down into the woods, meeting a well-defined track. Follow this for another 500 yds until it starts to bend sharply right, towards the main road, and take the footpath which follows the contours and runs parallel to the road.

After another 500 yds, take the footpath on the left running uphill, heading more or less S, which takes you to the minor road by Redmires Reservoir. Emerging on this, turn right and follow it round a left-hand bend.

Where the plantation on your right finishes, follow the lane around to the right, climbing SE to Stanedge Pole. Here bend slightly right and follow the path to Stanage Edge, turning left to follow the path which runs along the top, with spectacular views to your right.

*To shorten the walk, carry straight on along the road without entering the car park, as the route rejoins it by Redmires Reservoir in three-quarters of a mile.

At the trig point near the end of the edge, take the path which forks left, heading E to the road. Turn left on the road and cross the bridge over the head of the Burbage Brook. On your right you will see a lay-by, often with parked cars full of people admiring the view and drinking tea out of Thermos flasks. Take the second footpath on the right, and follow it along the top of Burbage Rocks, with more views. This leads you back to the A625. Turn left to get back to the Fox House.

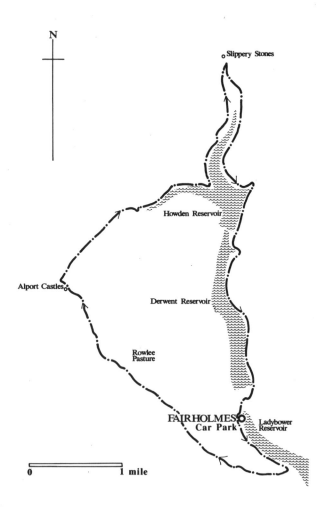

HAGGSIDE

Turning north from the A67 Glossop-Sheffield road 100 yds west of the Ashopton Viaduct brings you to one of the most touristy areas of the Peak District. There are car parks every couple of miles and lots of people sitting by the side of the road in deckchairs. It is not easy to forget, as you walk through trees and by the side of wide stretches of water here, that this is an almost entirely artificial landscape, not of lakes and forests, but of reservoirs and plantations. Why then is it so popular?

Well, the scenery, despite its artificiality, is not unattractive, and it's easy to get to – most of the deckchair people do not venture far. Despite the crowds down below, once out of the forest, walkers find themselves in beautiful, lonely, open moorland.

This walk starts from the Fairholmes car park two miles N of the A67. (You can also get here using the number 274 bus.)

WALK 1: Haggside-Birchin Hat-Slippery Stones

A relatively easy walk taking in moorland and some of the less crowded bits of forest and waterside.

Moderate then easy going, one climb.
11 miles, 4½ hrs.
Start SK173893.

Turn left out of the car park, heading S on the road, though you can take any of the footpaths down by the waterside, for three-quarters of a mile. You will then pass a four-square stone building on your left, and come to another car park on your right.

Just after the car park, take the footpath on the right, signposted as an old packhorse road to Glossop. This climbs uphill for half a mile and out of the plantation, where it meets another footpath. Turn right, keeping the trees you have just left on your right.

Over the crest of a small hill you come to a place where the path diverges. Carry straight on, directly uphill, and keep going uphill once into open country 350 yds later.

Two miles after having crossed into the open country you will find yourself able to see down into a steep-sided valley to your left. You are walking along the top of a rocky edge. This is Alport Castles: natural rock formations which look pretty spectacular from below, but there's not too much to see from up here.

Take the broad, well-defined track going off to the right, downhill, straight as a die to the NE. Almost a mile later this brings you back into the plantation and bends right. Keep heading downhill until you come to the road. Turn left.*

Follow the road around a long arm of the Howden Reservoir and as it bends N to its end. There is a kind of roundabout-in-the-middle-of-nowhere here, and a gate on the far side. Go through the gate, continuing for almost one more mile along the track.

This brings you out of the plantation to a place called Slippery Stones. Cross the river by the footbridge, and take the footpath on the right on the other side. This footpath follows the E side of the Howden and Derwent reservoirs for almost four miles.

At the second (the Derwent) dam, take the footpath which forks off to the right to a minor road (closed to traffic) and turn right back to the car park.

*You can shorten the walk here by turning right and following the road back to the car park (three-and-a-half miles).

The Only Grange path to Barker Bank (Castleton)

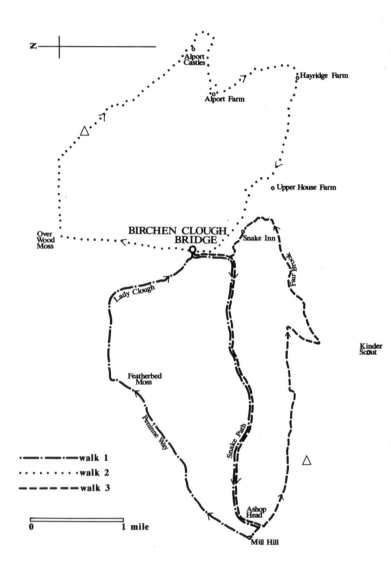

Alport Castles

Hayridge Farm

Alport Farm

Upper House Farm

BIRCHEN CLOUGH
BRIDGE

Snake Inn

Over
Wood
Moss

Lady Clough

Fair Brook

Featherbed
Moss

Kinder
Scout

Pennine Way

Snake Path

walk 1
walk 2
walk 3

Ashop
Head

0   1 mile

Mill Hill

HOPE FOREST

The name Hope Forest does not refer to the present plantation which lines the road, but to an older wilder area, only lightly wooded, which stretched over these moors and was mainly used as a hunting range. The forest is an ideal base for walking the moors to the north (Bleaklow) and south (Kinder), and there is a lot of really stunning country to be enjoyed, the vast majority of it open – you can wander at will. These walks all start from the car park by the side of the A57 at Birchen Clough Bridge.

WALK 1: Birchen Clough-Ashop Head-Featherbed Moss

A walk along valley bottoms which climbs gently on to the dramatic tops north of Kinder and which, despite going over rough country, is easy to follow. Check during the grouse season that the path is open.

Moderate and hard going with one gentle climb.
8 miles, 3 hrs.
Start SK109915.

Take the footpath opposite the car park W downhill into the Forestry Commission plantation. Follow this for 150 yds, down to a footbridge, and turn left, following the Commission's own walk waymarked in white and keeping to the left of the stream.

Proceed S for 600 yds, until you come to a footbridge across the stream. It was made from half a tree, and put there by the OTC, it says. Turn right and cross the stream. You are now on the Snake Path (an old packhorse road) and heading more or less due W, a course you will keep to for the next three miles.

Once you are out of the plantation you will be able to see that you are in a steep-sided clough with the huge, imposing bulk of Kinder Scout to your left. A relic of the area's past as a hunting range is the existence to your right of grouse butts, the hidey-holes people stand in when shooting birds.

You have been following the River Ashop (which flows down to the Ladybower Reservoir). After three miles both it and the path bend left, to the south. The river peters out (this is Ashop Head) and you meet the Pennine Way as it comes down off Kinder.

Follow the Pennine Way to the right and climb the hill. Pause to admire the views, then turn right once more and follow the Pennine Way NE along the ridge. There's a well-defined path and stakes, so this is easy.

After two-and-a-half miles the A57 heaves into view. Maintain a respectful distance from it (about 100 yds) and make your way to the right across country. There is no path, and the ground can be a bit soggy, but it's all good fun (though not necessarily very clean).

There is a stream which runs due E, parallel to the road, and it is a good idea to follow this, as it falls into a steep-sided clough by the roadside. You want to be at the bottom of that clough (Lady Clough). Follow it as it gets deeper and presently a rudimentary sort of path begins to appear on the left-hand side.

Follow this path and it will take you, as the clough bends S, back into the plantation. Cross the stile into the plantation and keep following the path by the side of the stream until you come to the first footbridge you crossed at the start of the walk. Turn left and climb back up to the car park.

WALK 2: Birchen Clough-Alport Castles-Cowms Moor

A moorland walk taking you up and over the high plateau to the very dramatic natural rock formation of Alport Castles and back through a pleasant wooded valley. The high ground covered is mainly peat bog, so make sure your feet are well protected. There is no path on the ground for much of the way, so have a compass with you and do not attempt the walk in poor visibility.

Hard going, one long, one short, steep climb.
9 miles, 4 hrs.
Start SK109905.

At the back of the car park take the footpath heading straight uphill N. At the stile marking the boundary of the open country keep going uphill. You are making for the highest point of this hill and, as a rough guide, the bearing is about 10 degrees.

Once the ground starts to level off you will be able to see where you are going – a very gentle rise just a few degrees E of N. Once at the highest point stop and look E. There is a trig point on top of the hill opposite (bearing 115 degrees) and it is for this that you are now going to make.

Since, however, there is a valley in between you and the trig point, it will be easier if you head off due E, making your way across the head of Alport Dale, and up the other side, turning SE when the ground levels out (at which point you should be able to see the trig point again) rather than heading straight for it, as the valley is easier to cross at this point.

Having reached the trig point (by whatever means) take the footpath SE, parallel to the valley. You will soon find yourself walking along the lip of the valley, looking down on to rows and rows of pine trees. After a mile Alport Castles can be seen below you to the right. This is not, however, the best angle to appreciate them from.

At the other end of the castles the footpath bends right, over a stile, and heads downhill. Now is the time to start turning around and looking at the rocks – they look more impressive the further down you go.

At the bottom of the valley cross the river by the footbridge and follow the path as it bends left, following the valley S. You are now on a farm lane heading for the main road.

After a mile, the lane forks. Take the right fork to Hayridge Farm, forking right again once you get there (i.e. not going down on to the main road). This footpath follows the course of the original Roman road through the Snake Pass, though there is nothing to see of it, and runs above and roughly parallel to the A57 for two-and-a-half miles before entering the plantation and joining the A57 300 yds S of the car park. (Turn right on to the road.)

WALK 3: Birchen Clough-Ashop Head-Kinder-Fairbrook Clough

A simple circle taking you on to the less fashionable, but rewarding, northern edge of Kinder Scout.

Moderate going, one long, gentle climb.
9 miles, 4 hrs.
Start SK109905.

Follow Walk 1 to the Pennine Way at Ashop Head. Turn left and follow the Way up on to Kinder. Just before the first big group of boulders, 300 yds later, take the footpath branching off left, which climbs gently on to the edge of the plateau and runs parallel to the Snake Path and Ashop Clough.

Follow the edge of the plateau for the better part of two miles, until it turns sharply inwards, to the S. Follow it for another 700 yds until it turns back to the E. Here, turn sharply left, back on yourself, and make your way down the clough heading ENE towards the Snake Road.

There is a path which follows the stream, Fair Brook, though if it is wet weather the going can be very squelchy in places. If it is dry, though, this can be a surprisingly lush and pleasant little valley, and even in the winter it does have its attractions, especially if you've just come down off Kinder and there's a north wind raging, as it is quite sheltered. A good place for a snack and a sit down, maybe.

The footpath winds along the bottom of the clough for over a mile-and-a-half. At the mouth of the clough, head left making for a stile 100 yds further on which gives on to a footbridge over the River Ashop.

On the other side of the bridge is a footpath which takes you up on to the road. Follow it and turn left, going past the Snake Inn. After another 250 yds, take the footpath on the left, down into the plantation. This will bring you back to the half-a-tree/OTC footbridge you crossed on your way out. Turn right and retrace your steps back to the car park.

BRADFIELD

There are two villages here. High Bradfield is halfway up the moorside. Low Bradfield, unsurprisingly, is lower down. Both have a great deal of charm, and are totally different in character from the villages of the Derbyshire Peak just a few miles to the south. This, after all, is Yorkshire, where the men are men and everyone else is a Jessie.

WALK 1: Strines-Back Tor-Smallfield

A moorland walk with a pleasant, lowland finish. There are paths on the ground for most of the way, but it is still an extremely good idea when attempting a walk over this terrain to make sure you have a compass. This walk starts from the car park (unofficial, but easy to find) which is the first turning to the left on the northern side of the steep, sharp bend north of the Strines Inn.

Moderate going, one climb.
11½ miles, 5 hrs.
Start SK221909.

At the end of this wide bit of asphalt, take the signposted lane climbing NNW through the trees. It soon bends WSW and starts to climb more steeply.

Once out of the plantation, keep climbing in the same direction until you find yourself, a mile later, unable to climb any further as you've run out of hill. Turn right and make for the trig point at the very top.

The path forks here. Go right. (That cairn at the end of the ridge to the left is called Lost Lad, the story being that a young shepherd from the now drowned village of Derwent got lost up here in a blizzard and, finding what shelter he could, laid down to die. When they found his body some time later he had carved the words 'Lost Lad' on the rocks.)

This path continues for almost two miles, heading NNE then due N, before being joined by another coming up a clough from the left. Bend NNE, following a clough which is beginning on your right.

Once the clough is behind you, the path swings around E, to the right, and begins to descend, gently, the spur of moor on the north side of the clough. It comes out on to a road which you will be able to see from quite a way away.

Across the road is the Bar Dyke, an iron-age fortification, though it is not very exciting to look at. Turn right on the road and follow it S. Carry on past the road off to the left, around a very tight bend and up a steep hill.

After three-quarters of a mile you come to another turning to the left (with signs advertising farmhouse B&B). Carry straight on again, taking the footpath on the left (signposted) 100 yds later.

This takes you downhill to another road. Turn right, along a charming wooded lane, bending right, then left, 500 yds later, past a farm. At another right bend, take the footpath straight on, to a lane which runs by the side of the reservoir.

Past the dam of the next reservoir, the lane bends right and starts to climb uphill, emerging at a gate on to the road. Turn left and follow the road around to the right to come back to the car park. Time for a pint in the Strines – it has good beer and a selection of specially stuffed wild animals.

WALK 2: Smallfield-Derwent-Moscar-Moor Lodge

Sheer distance, and the amount of climbing involved, make this a hard walk. It is not too difficult to find your way as there are paths on the ground, but you need to be fit to attempt it. It starts from the National Trust's car park at Smallfield, two miles NW of Bradfield on the Strines-Midhopestones road.

Two gentle climbs, one severe.
17 miles, 8 hrs.
Start SK246946.

On the other side of the road from the car park, take the signposted footpath on to the moors and up Round Hill – you can see the line of the path gently bending round to the south following the clough on your left as you start.

After three miles of gentle climbing, the clough to your left finally peters out, and another appears to your right. Take the path on the right (not very distinct) which descends it. Keep to the left side of the clough – you will start off heading SW before heading WNW, but by this time you will be on a track.

This brings you down, through a plantation, to the track running by the side of the Derwent Reservoir. Take it to the left for almost two miles, until it joins a metalled lane, and turn half-left on to this, past some houses.

After another mile, the lane bends left and crosses an inlet before resuming its previous heading. After another 400 yds, two tracks go off to the left. Take the second of these, over a stile, and climb steeply uphill, following the small clough on your right-hand side.

Over another stile and the path bends right, crossing the clough and climbing to the left of a plantation to meet another wall higher up the hill.

Here it turns right and, soon after, forks. Fork left, climbing steeply. This takes you to the crest of the hill, more than 800 feet higher than you were when you started this climb. The panorama from the top is magnificent.

Heading due E now, descend gently for just over a mile, until you reach a lane leading to a square, isolated stone-built farmhouse. Take this to the left and follow it past the house (Moscar House) to the road.

You emerge at a fork. Take the turning on the right, signposted to Ughill, past the pumping station. Follow this road for three-quarters of a mile, until you come to the gates of Sugworth Hall on the left. Turn down the drive.

The footpath branches off to the right after 300 yds, skirting the house to the right and heading well to the right of the folly tower standing on the promontory overlooking the reservoir.

At the valley bottom take the footpath on the left over the back of the dam of Strines Reservoir on to a lane on the other side. Turn right, following this lane on to a minor road, turning left at the end of the woods to avoid the farmyard.

Turn right on to the road, following it round a right-hand then a left-hand bend. Pass a footpath sign on your right, then take the footpath on the left steeply uphill, to emerge close to a fork in the road to Smallfield. Take the fork on the left and follow the road back to the car park (three-quarters of a mile).

WALK 3: Low Bradfield-Onesmoor

A short walk exploring both Bradfields and part of the surrounding moor, this walk is an illustration of how landscape changes as you move vertically – it climbs almost 900 feet. It starts from Low Bradfield, where there is ample parking.

Easy-moderate going with one climb.
4½ miles, 2 hrs.
Start SK262922.

From Bradfield's main street take the lane which runs alongside the cricket pitch, school and tennis courts (and the toilet block on the other side). After the tennis courts cross a footbridge and take the footpath on the right uphill.

As it climbs it crosses Moorfield Lane and comes into High Bradfield past the church. Turn left on to the lane and emerge on the main street. The footpath on to the moor is opposite and slightly left.

Cross another road on to open pasture and follow the path to the trig point on the top of Onesmoor. From here there is what would be a magnificent view to the east if it weren't for Sheffield. The path goes on slightly to the left, heading to the right of a scrubby wood and a radio mast (the small, nearer one).

This brings you down the left-hand side of a wall on to a road.

Turn right to a crossroads, then right again. After 400 yds cross the wooden stile over a wire fence. You can see the footpath descending due S.

The path comes out on to a road to the right of the grounds of a convent. Turn right past Primrose Farm Cottage and the entrance to Fair Flats Farm, taking the next footpath on the left. As you approach a farm, take the lane on the right on to the road and, once on the road, turn right back into High Bradfield. From here, retrace your steps to Low Bradfield.

Below Hollins Cross (Castleton)

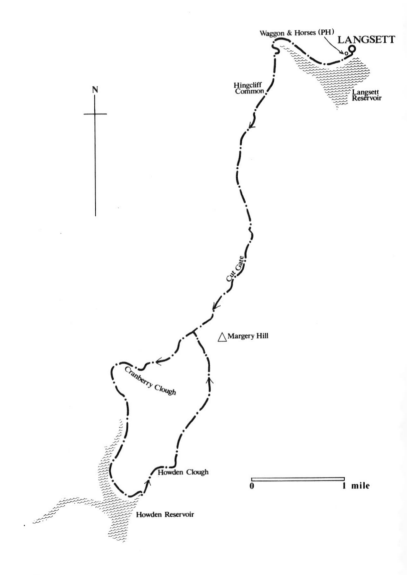

LANGSETT

There's nothing much to Langsett beyond the Waggon and Horses, a Youth Hostel, a few houses, the busy A616 and a car park, but it is close to some superb moorland. Non car-drivers can get here by bus from Sheffield and Manchester.

WALK 1: Langsett-Margery Hill-Howden-Margery Hill

A long moorland walk which has the huge advantage of starting and finishing at a pub.

Moderate going with a lot of climbing.
14 miles, 7 hrs.
Start SE212005.

Take the footpath 50 yds to the right of the Waggon and Horses. This runs along the edge of the Forestry Commission plantation for half a mile, then enters it.

After another half-mile it meets a broad, well-defined track. Turn left, emerging from the plantation 150 yds later and crossing a small stream.

You now start to climb, heading a few degrees west of south, over the boundary of open country. At the next stile, branch right and continue climbing, now heading south of SW. The path takes you down over a broad clough, back out of the open country, and on to Mickleden Edge – the top of a steep slope down into a lightly wooded clough on your right.

Follow the path S then SW, gently uphill, a further two miles until the ground starts to fall away. You will be able to see two trig points – right and left. Now descend SW for a further mile, until you find yourself in a deep valley aligned N-S.

At the bottom the path meets another. Turn left and follow it alongside the stream, forking left when it splits after 200 yds. This takes you alongside the Howden Reservoir for a mile-and-a-half.

The path then bends sharply left then right, and there is a signposted footpath on the left climbing a clough out of the forest. Follow it, heading NW. The clough bends W to its head. At a scrubby wood climb the northern side of the clough, heading due N until the land flattens out. Then follow the lie of the land NW, climbing N again when the side of the hill on your right comes around to meet you.

This brings you back to the path you came on. Turn right and retrace your steps to Langsett.

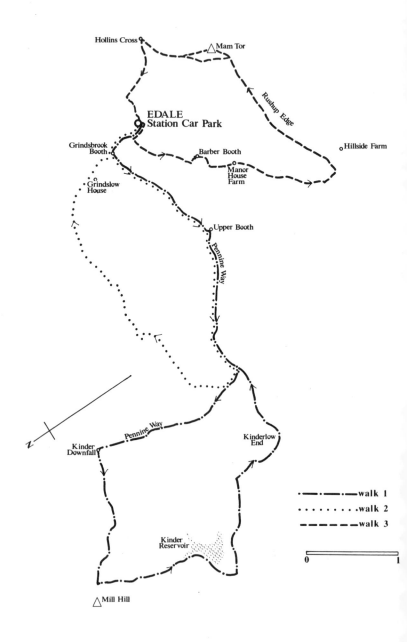

THE NORTH-WEST

EDALE

As the starting point of the Pennine Way, and being right underneath Kinder Scout, Edale is very popular with walkers. It is misleading to speak of it as one village – it is several spread out over the whole length of the valley between the Mam Tor-Lose Hill ridge and Kinder, but the centre of it is the road north from the valley road (past the railway station), where there are several houses, a church, an information centre for the National Park and two pubs. At the junction of the two roads there is a sizable car park, where these walks start.

WALK 1: Edale-Jacob's Ladder-Ashop Head-Edale Cross

One of the hardest walks in the book, this requires a great deal of stamina as it has a taxing climb after a quarter of its distance and another three-quarters of the way through. The rewards, though, are considerable. Besides the feeling of achievement, it does manage to cover a variety of scenery unusual in this part of the Dark Peak.

Hard going, two long hard climbs.
15½ miles, 7 hrs.*
Start SK124853.

Turn right on to the village road and follow it under the railway bridge and past the Ramblers Inn and the church. When you have walked almost half a mile you will come to the Nag's Head. Take the footpath on the left, which used to be the start of the Pennine Way (there is now an alternative route). The path goes past a few cottages and into a sunken lane (wet in winter, fly-infested at other times).

At the end of this, cross the stile. The path forks. Go left, and follow it across fields for a mile and a bit, until you come to Upper Booth, one of the Edale villages (though not much more than a farm and a few cottages).

You can shorten this walk by three miles by parking in the car park at Barber Booth and following the road left (NE) to Upper Booth to join the route there.

The path bends left through the farmyard and on to a lane. Turn right and follow it as it bends left then right to a gate. Go through this, following the sign for Lee Farm, and up the valley ENE on a broad track.

This continues all very pleasantly for a mile. Then the track comes to an old packhorse bridge. Cross this, turning left, and start the long, steep climb up Jacob's Ladder.

After the climb (and the pain) has eased off a bit, you will come to a wall where the path forks. Go right (NNE) with the Pennine Way, still climbing. Now you come to the only tricky bit of navigation on the walk – the path on the ground bends around to the right, but you need to keep heading NNE and keep climbing, over Kinder Low, the highest point in the Peak District. There are cairns to mark the way, and the trig point is a useful point of reference if you can see it.

You will then come to the western perimeter of Kinder. Follow it. There's no path, but it is easy to find your way as you simply have to keep the sharp drop to your left. A mile of this and you come to Kinder Downfall, where the River Kinder sometimes falls over the edge of the plateau, sometimes blows back in your face and often isn't there at all.

The edge here takes a severe left turn and you are now heading WNW. The small pool on the hillside below you, by the way (not the reservoir, the smaller one) is called Mermaid's Pool because there is a mermaid living in it. But you can, the story goes, only see her at midnight on Easter Sunday. So, no luck there, then.

Follow the edge for a further mile until you start to descend past some rocky outcrops into a valley, where you can see a path going up the other side. At the lowest point of this descent, take the path on the left down the clough which starts here. It's called William Clough ('Brian' would have been funnier, if wildly inappropriate). Follow it all the way down – it is occasionally difficult going and you have to cross and re-cross the stream.

Eventually you will come out by the Kinder Reservoir. Follow the path along the right side of it, climbing through the bracken before you get to the dam. After this, where the path forks, go left into the bottom of the valley, turning left again on to a farm lane.

A hundred-and-fifty yards later, where this meets another lane, take the footpath opposite, heading off to the right, uphill, alongside the plantation. This will bring you to the stile giving on to open country. Take the footpath on the right. Aim to head S for about half a mile, then follow the path up and around to the left, to join a lane along a clough running ENE to its head.

This is the old packhorse route from Edale to Hayfield and will take you to Edale Cross (a re-erected medieval stone) and back to Jacob's Ladder, from where all you have to do is retrace your steps to Edale and the Nag.

WALK 2: Edale-Jacob's Ladder-Grindsbrook Clough

A simple, but taxing, walk which makes use of the two divergent routes taken by the Pennine Way out of Edale and allows you to climb on to Kinder without having to do too much complicated navigating. Do not, however, venture up there without the right equipment, including a compass.

Hard going, one hard climb.
8 miles, 3½ hrs.
Start SK124853.

Follow Walk 1 past the top of Jacob's Ladder and the right turn at the wall. Stay on the path as it bends around to the right. You will be heading NNE at this point, and will gradually swing around to a more easterly direction as you follow the path on to the southern edge of the plateau.

You will be able to see down into the valley you came up, and ahead of you and to the right, on the other side of the Vale of Edale, is Mam Tor. Keep heading E for half a mile, until you cross the top of a spur of the plateau sticking out below you. The path here bends left slightly, going NE for a few hundred yards before reaching the edge again and resuming its eastwards course once it has rounded the head of a clough falling away SSE.

A further three-quarters of a mile of heading E will take you over another spur to the edge of Grindsbrook Clough. Make your way down this, still heading E – there is a path, but it can be a bit slippery. The path keeps more or less to the bottom of the clough as it bends around to the right and ends up heading SSE.

You will then, after a mile of this, come to a stile. The footpath on the other side leads through some trees and back to Edale, bending right to cross the brook half a mile after the stile.

WALK 3: Edale-Barber Booth-Rushup-Hollins Cross

A magnificent ridgewalk follows a stiffish climb. This walk is, perhaps, best not done by those who want solitude in their walking, at least not on summer weekends, as there is a car park near the top of the ridge and bits of it can get crowded.

Moderate going, one hard climb.
7½ miles, 3 hrs.
Start SK124853.

Turn right from the car park into Edale as before, but take the first footpath on the left (clearly signposted to Barber Booth) after the Rambler's Rest. This follows a lane for a while, then heads across fields and a bridge over the railway before turning left on to the valley road at Barber Booth.

On the road turn right, then take the next turning right, signposted to Upper Booth. Two hundred yards along this road, take the signposted footpath on the left climbing gently over fields to the right of a farm. The path then joins a well-defined track – Chapel Gate, the old Edale-Chapel-en-le-Frith packhorse route.

The path climbs quite severely SW on to open moorland. At the top of the steep bit of the climb it crosses a wall and bends left, to head more directly S. Where it meets the next wall, join the track running along your side of the wall and turn left.

You are now atop Rushup Edge. Follow the ridge for the next mile-and-a-half as it rises over Lord's Seat, the highest point, and dips down towards Mam Tor.

Coming out on to the road, take the footpath opposite and to the right, straight to the top of the hill. Pause at the trig point for a look around, then continue along the ridge for another three-quarters of a mile.

This brings you to Hollins Cross, where there is a cairn and several paths meet – it can get a bit like a hill-top motorway interchange here in the busy season. Take the footpath on the left which goes downhill diagonally and back on the way you've come. Before long bend right and follow the wall on your right downhill, passing to the left of the farm in front of you on to a track. This will take you to the road where turning left will bring you back to Edale.

Castleton from Hollins Cross

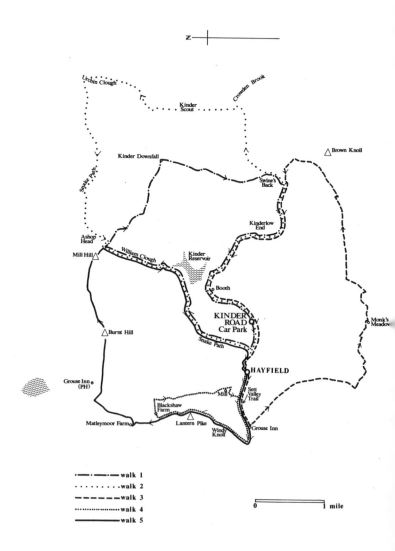

HAYFIELD

A pleasant little village on the western edge of the High Peak, Hayfield nestles underneath Kinder Scout and is a Mecca for walkers. It has a number of good pubs (try the Kinder Lodge, the George and the Sportsman) and a great deal of quaintness, though it does betray its proximity to Manchester in places with a few disturbingly suburban streets.

Walks 1 and 2 start from the car park at Bowden Bridge, at the far end of Kinder Road (as far as car drivers are concerned). It has a monument to the mass trespass on Kinder which started from here and which was so instrumental in opening the area up to walkers.

The other walks all start from the car park (signposted, just off the A624) at the east end of the new Sett Valley Trail, one of the Peak's many former railways turned into footpaths.

WALK 1: Snake Path-Ashop Head-Kinder-Edale Cross

The classic western approach to Kinder Scout, this is a hard walk, though a rewarding one – the western edge of Kinder Scout is extremely dramatic, and the surrounding moors are dominated by it.

Moderate going, hard climbing.
10 miles, 4½ hrs.
Start SK049869.

Turn right out of the car park on to Kinder Road. Pass the pub, and a quarter of a mile later turn right on to the Snake Path – it is signposted, and climbs steeply uphill – and follow it as it bends left and climbs rather gently on to the low moors below Kinder.

After three-quarters of a mile, at the boundary of open country, the path bends right and begins to head more directly towards Kinder, still climbing, as it runs alongside Kinder Reservoir.

As the path bends left, away from the reservoir, and starts to follow William Clough, things get a little harder. There is a long climb now up to Ashop Head, where you meet the Pennine Way at the head of the clough.

Turn right here and climb the spur of Kinder, past the groups of boulders and try to keep to the right-hand edge of the plateau. There is no distinct path, but you will be able to see the reservoir below you to the right and you will be heading SE most of the time. You deserve a rest, by the way. Pause to reflect that you have climbed about 1,500 feet since you left Hayfield.

After a mile-and-a-half of dodging boulders and working your way along the edge of the plateau, you come to Kinder Downfall. This is nominally a waterfall, but in summer there is frequently no water in it, and in other seasons, when the wind is from the W or SW (i.e. most of the time) the water does not so much fall as spray back in your face.

Here the edge you are following changes direction, bending right through nearly 90 degrees and heading SSW, but stick with it. Almost two miles later you will be able to see a trig point, and then you run out of plateau.

Begin your descent, and you will encounter a path running across your way. Take it to the right, over the Swine's Back (a distinctive hummock, and an annoying false summit when seen from the south), keeping to the right side of a low stone wall.

This will take you to Edale Cross. Take the footpath on the right, pausing to see if you can decipher any of the hieroglyphics on the cross itself (it's a medieval stone, re-erected last century). This footpath heads W, descending gently, before swinging N and following a wall for 500 yds.

There is then a stile on your left (on the other side of one of the National Trust's open country signs). Climb over it and follow the path downhill to join a track heading for the woods at the bottom of the hill, where the track bends left.

Where the track forks, after leaving the field, fork left and you are back on Kinder Road. This goes S, then SW for a mile-and-a-half, back to Hayfield.

WALK 2: Edale Cross-Crowden Falls-Fairbrook Clough-Snake Path

Covering similar territory to Walk 1, this is a harder, hairier walk which involves navigating across Kinder Scout by compass. Expect to be completely knackered at the end of this one however fit you might think you are. Do not attempt this walk without a) a compass and b) knowing how to use it, as you will get lost. It is also advisable not to attempt it in poor visibility.

Hard going, one long climb.
13 miles, 6 hrs.
Start SK049869.

Turn left out of the car park on to Kinder Road and follow it for the best part of a mile until it forks. Take the right fork uphill to a crossroads, and take the track on the right. This runs through a field by the side of some scrawny-looking woods, though it soon bends diagonally away to the right, heading more seriously uphill and down grading into a footpath.

This path brings you to the boundary of open country. Climb over the stile and follow the footpath on the right, hugging the wall. The wall falls away and, 400 yds later, the path bends around to the left, still climbing but now through rugged, open country, and you find yourself on a well-defined lane.

Half a mile later you come to Edale Cross. Turn left and follow the footpath by the wall, heading uphill and NE. Once the climb has eased off a little you are practically at the top. You are on a well-trodden path which is starting to swing around (E) right and below you to your right you can see down into the Vale of Edale. Mam Tor is visible to the SE.

Follow this course for another half mile, past a spur of Kinder jutting out below you, until a clough appears in the hillside ahead of you and the path veers to the left.

Go to the head of the clough, where the path resumes its previous course. This is where things get tricky: strike off N, away from the track, into the vast, trackless wilderness. You need to be heading due N, and checking your compass frequently to make sure you are not wandering off course (and, given the number of obstacles, groughs and meres, it is very easy to wander). More than a mile later (it will feel like six) you will reach the other side of the plateau.

If you have been true to the bearing you will be at the head of another clough, Fairbrook Clough, running roughly NE. If, looking downhill, you can see a busy main road running left and right, you have strayed too far east; if you can see a deep, straight clough running parallel to the perimeter of the plateau, too far west.

Follow the left-hand side of the clough down off the plateau. You will notice after some 500 yds that the ground on this side of the clough begins to level out for a short while. Take this opportunity to move away from the clough, heading N over the flatter piece of ground, and then down into the clough running E-W in front of you.

Follow this clough W, either finding a way across the stream on to the Snake Path, or staying on the S side of it, for two miles to Ashop Head. Here the clough bends SW and finishes. Go over its head and follow the Snake Path down William Clough to Kinder Reservoir.

The Snake Path will lead you back to Hayfield, though it is marginally quicker and easier to make your way down to the path running by the side of the reservoir (bearing in mind there is no right of access here except on designated footpaths) and follow it SW on to Kinder Road.

WALK 3: Sett Valley Trail-Birch Vale-Chinley Churn-Edale Cross

A hard walk with a lot of climbing, but a rewarding one which covers a variety of terrain.

Moderate going, two climbs.
11½ miles, 5 hrs.
Start SK036869.

Take the Sett Valley Trail W for one mile until you meet a road. Turn left. At the end of this road cross the main street and take the steeply climbing lane left of the Grouse Inn, which leads SE on to a footpath to the top of Chinley Churn.

Follow this path for almost two miles, until it flattens out and then descends slightly. When you come to a lane off right, take the footpath on the left uphill, and descend steeply the other side. You can see where you are going from here – over the main road on the other side of the valley and up the big hill in front of you and slightly left.

At a minor road, turn left and take the first right, continuing down to the bottom of the valley and up to the road on the other side. You emerge almost opposite the Lamb Inn. Just to the right of it, take the signposted (though the sign gets hidden by vegetation) footpath uphill from the grassy verge.

After three fields, this path meets another. Turn left and head NE, coming to a stile and the boundary of open country. Cross over and follow the footpath on the right, heading due E. Follow this path (it's quite distinct) for two miles, climbing the long shoulder of Brown Knoll, and gradually turning northwards.

A few hundred yards after starting to descend northwards, you meet a path coming from the right with, very often, quite a lot of red-faced, knackered people on it. This is the Pennine Way at the head of Jacob's Ladder (one of the most arduous climbs in the Peak). Pause to gloat.

Take the footpath on the left, alongside a wall. This becomes a lane, half a mile further on, and forks as it is crossing a clough diagonally. Take the right fork, and follow it around to the N.

Five hundred yards later the path is running alongside a wall and then there is a stile on the left. Climb over it and take the footpath descending NW to a wood, where it bends left.

Where the track forks, after leaving the field, fork left and you are back on Kinder Road. The road goes S, then SW for a mile-and-a-half, back to Hayfield and those pubs.

WALK 4: Sett Valley Trail-Birch Vale-Lantern Pike

A charming little walk which wanders a rich valley landscape and pokes its head out on to open moorland. This is definitely one to take your field guides to wild flowers and birds on.

Easy going, one climb.
5 miles, 2½ hrs.
Start SK036869.

Take the Sett Valley Trail W from the car park for one mile to the old level crossing at Birch Vale. Turn right on to the road, past a curious cafe in a hut which does surprisingly good cakes, and over the river. Past a row of houses dated 1854 (the Crescent – artisans' houses from the days when this was the cotton capital of the world), take the steep cobbled lane on the right.

Carry straight on, uphill, where the lane forks, and emerge opposite a row of houses called Windy Knoll. Take the lane to the right of these, still climbing. In spring in this lane there is a riot of wild flowers, in summer a pestilence of midges.

Passing a farmhouse on your left, you cross a stile into the National Trust property on top of Lantern Pike. Suddenly the landscape has changed – this is open, uncultivated. The wild flowers are smaller, upland types. From the very top of the hill the view is intriguing – look east and you see dramatic, high empty hills. Look west and there's Manchester. On the whole it's probably better to look east.

The footpath leads you down off Lantern Pike diagonally across a field to a signpost where five paths meet. Follow the sign to Carr Meadow and Edale (rightish), downhill to a farm. Skirt this to the left and proceed in the same direction.

Further downhill, take the footpath on the right, which is signposted to Little Hayfield and runs due S. This takes you though a natural wood, past mills and cottages and, three-quarters of a mile later, past a pool (downhill to the left) which is home to a pair of herons.

Shortly after this, the path forks. Go left, which brings you out into Swallowhouse Lane. At the end of this (Swallowhouse Hall on the right has now been converted into highly des. lux. apts, by the way) turn right past the school, taking the asphalted lane on the left immediately before the bridge. This takes you back to the Sett Valley Trail. Turn left to get back to the car park.

WALK 5: Sett Valley Trail-Lantern Pike-Abbott's Chair-Burnt Hill

There is a tremendous variety of landscapes on this walk – quaint post-industrial, low natural woodland, pasture and high, wild moors.

Moderate going with two climbs, one of them long.
9½ miles, 4 hrs.
Start SK036869.

Follow Walk 4 over Lantern Pike to the signpost at the meeting of five paths, taking the one to Matley Moor (straight on). This goes along a lane and comes to a farm after 50 yds. Turn right here, along a lane, then 200 yds later, left down another. After half a mile, this will lead you down a wide land on to a road. You come out opposite a farm which is patrolled, the signs say, by ferocious dogs.

This road is called Monks' Road, after the monks who built and owned it, and the little knoll is called Abbots Chair, after the abbot who sat on it (or, rather, for some less tangible reason). Turn right to take you to the main road.

The Grouse Inn is to your left, and opposite there is a stile giving on to open country. Cross the stile and follow the footpath on the other side uphill for two miles. It's a gentle climb, but it's long and wearying.

At the highest point yet, where you meet a staked path coming from the left, head downhill to the bottom of the dip between this hill (Mill Hill) and Kinder Scout. There turn right on to the Snake Path, which will lead you SSW to Hayfield via Kinder Reservoir (see Walk 2).

Old Dam (Peak Forest)

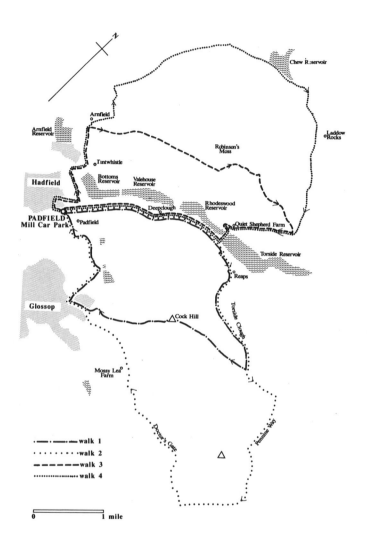

Chew Reservoir

Arnfield

Arnfield
Reservoir

Laddow
Rocks

Tintwhistle

Robinson's
Moss

Bottoms
Reservoir

Valehouse
Reservoir

Hadfield

Deepclough

Rhodeswood
Reservoir

Quiet Shepherd Farm

PADFIELD
Mill Car Park

Padfield

Torside Reservoir

Reaps

Glossop

Torside Clough

Cock Hill

Mossy Lea
Farm

Doctor's Gate

Pennine Way

walk 1
walk 2
walk 3
walk 4

0   1 mile

PADFIELD

Still a village, despite almost being swallowed up by the Manchester/ Glossop urban sprawl. It is perched right on the edge of a massive city, but within walking distance of Bleaklow and Longdendale. These walks all start from the car park at the end of the old Longdendale railway – follow signs to Hadfield Station, then follow Platt St past the Palatine Arms. The car park is on the left immediately before the railway bridge. The walks could just as easily be used by non car-users by taking the train to Hadfield.

WALK 1: Padfield-Torside-Cock Hill-Old Glossop

Using the old railway to get into the heart of Longdendale, this walk then climbs almost to the top of Bleaklow before cutting across wild moorland and descending into Old Glossop, covering a bewildering variety of sceneries. The walk involves traversing country with no paths, so do not attempt in bad weather.

Moderate and hard going, one substantial climb.
10 miles, 4½ hrs.
Start SK025963.

Follow the old railway NE through its deep cutting out of Padfield and on to the southern side of Longdendale. This might be the time to start speculating about a local mystery – there has been a lot of controversy in the Peak District local papers, and elsewhere, over recent years, about mysterious lights seen in the sky in this area. They are known, not very mysteriously, as 'the Longdendale Lights'. Look out for a local with a very powerful torch. (I favour the car headlights theory, myself.)

After almost three miles of old railway you are ready to turn off. There is an old level crossing, and the Pennine Way runs over the track. Turn right on to the road – the Way goes off up the hill 50 yds back down the road.

A steep and arduous climb brings you up on to the eastern edge of Peaknaze Moor. Follow the edge first S, climbing, then E, on the level. The Way then bends S again, and the depth of the clough to your left diminishes rapidly until there is hardly anything to it.

Now take the footpath on the right, heading due W. Follow it until you can see a trig point ahead of you and slightly left, then make for that across country. (If the weather has closed in, keeping on the western heading for just over half a mile will take you downhill to a track running alongside a wall. Turn left and you will rejoin the route.)

From the trig point take the footpath which leads away downhill

SW to the entrance to a lane. Following this lane as it bends right and passes a plantation will bring you down into Old Glossop.

At the end of the lane, amongst the houses, turn right on to Hope Lane. At the end of this, turn right on to Wellgate (with its attractive line of pubs) and right again on to Blackshaw Road. You are now looking for a small cul-de-sac called Castle Hill, at the end of which is an overgrown lane running due N for half a mile to Swineshaw Reservoir.

At the reservoir, take the footpath on the left to the road. Turn right on the road, taking the footpath on the left past a farmhouse 70 yds later. When, after 600 yds, you come to a larger farm, take the footpath on the left, which will bring you out on the corner of Platt St in Padfield. Turn right and follow it back to the car park.

WALK 2: Padfield-Torside-Doctor's Gate-Old Glossop

Extending Walk 1, this walk goes up and over the summit of Bleaklow, well over 2,000 feet high, and returns over wild moorland by an old Roman road.

Moderate-hard going with a long hard climb.
13 miles, 6 hrs.
Start SK025963.

Follow Walk 1 on to the Pennine Way, but instead of turning off at Torside, stay on the Way all the way to the top of Bleaklow. This is a hard and exhausting climb because it goes on for so long and because of the nature of the ground.

At the point where Walk 1 and this walk diverge, there are various paths. As long as you keep going uphill, all will get you to the right place. At Bleaklow Head, the top of the hill, have a look around – you can see for miles – and head due S.

After almost five miles of the most rugged and exhilarating moorland in the Peak District, as the Pennine Way descends to cross the A57 Snake Road, take the Doctor's Gate path on the right down along a clough.

This path leads W then NW down off the moor into farming country, becoming a more well-defined lane. Where it forks near a reservoir, take the right fork. This will bring you out, a mile later, by a factory in Old Glossop.

Turn right past the bus-turning area, and then take the second turning on the left (Hope Lane). At the end, turn right into Wellgate, right again immediately into Blackshaw Road (unless you stop for a pint in the Wheatsheaf), and take the footpath from the end of Castle Hill to Swineshaw Reservoir.

At the reservoir, take the footpath on the left to the road. Turn right on the road, taking the footpath on the left past a farmhouse 70 yds later. When, after 600 yds, you come to a larger farm, take the footpath on the left, which will bring you out on the corner of Platt St in Padfield. Turn right and follow it back to the car park.

WALK 3: Padfield-Tintwistle-Quiet Shepherd

This walk explores both sides of Longdendale, and its climbing is done quite gradually though it does ascend more than 1,000 feet.

Moderate going, one long gentle climb.
9½ miles, 4 hrs.
Start SK025963.

Go out of the car park on to the road and turn right, following it round a right-hand bend past the Palatine on to Station Road. Turn right into Lambgates (opposite the pub on the corner of Kiln Lane) and follow the footpath at the end to Padfield Main Road.

Turn left on the road and follow it for 700 yds, past the One Way sign and the pumping station, and downhill on to Tintwistle (pron. Tinsel) Bridge. Turn right and on the other side of the bridge right again, on to Bank Lane.

Follow this uphill and you come out on to Tintwistle High Street next to the church. Take the small lane uphill opposite, past the village stocks, and on to a back street. Opposite and to your left, follow Arnfield Lane, leading gently uphill past an assortment of allotments, garages, sheds etc.

You pass a turning off to the left, and 600 yds further on, a group of farm buildings on your right. Just past these, take the footpath on the right, leading uphill on to the moor. After 500 yds you pass the boundary of the open country and the path becomes a well-defined track running more or less NE, then ENE, for two miles.

Once it is right on the lip of the hill and you are looking down a very steep slope and over the reservoirs of Longdendale to your right, the track bends sharply left to climb the remaining 200 feet to the top of the hill, where it resumes its previous course.

Very soon, though, after crossing a clough, it bends right again and begins to descend, gently at first, then more steeply, eventually coming to another footpath running along the side of a low stone wall. Turn right and follow the path SW to meet the main road.

Turn right on the road and take the next turning left, after a farmhouse, and then go through the stile on the left side of this gently sloping lane. You are now on a path which takes you over the reservoir. Once on the other side, simply follow the path left for 100 yds and then turn sharply right on to the old railway to take you back to Padfield.

WALK 4: Padfield-Tintwistle-Chew-Crowden Clough-Quiet Shepherd

This walk may set out from very close to the suburbs of Manchester, but it covers some wild territory, though there are paths on the ground all the way.

Moderate going, one long climb.
12 miles, 5 hrs.
Start SK025963.

Follow Walk 3 on to Arnfield Lane, but instead of turning right, follow it to the farm at the end.

Take the lane which goes uphill right (signposted to open country), forking left when it splits 500 yds later (follow the wall on your left). At the end of the wall 300 yds later, strike off due N into the bottom of the clough, then follow the wall up the other side. You will soon meet a well-defined path. Take it to the right, heading NNE.

Stay on this path for over two miles as it turns gradually eastwards, eventually hugging the lip of Chew Clough and coming to Chew Reservoir.

Take the path E along the S side of the reservoir, and follow it a further mile across open moorland. Bleak, isn't it? You will now meet the Pennine Way at Laddow Rocks – you are heading SE and descending sharply into the bottom of a wide, deep clough.

After a mile and a half of this, you reach the boundary of the open country. Take the path straight on and follow it SW to meet the main road.

Turn right on the road and take the next turning left, after a farmhouse, and then go through the stile on the left side of this gently sloping lane. You are now on a path which takes you over the reservoir. Once on the other side, simply follow the path left for 100 yds and then turn sharply right on to the old railway to take you back to Padfield.

Climbing to Hollins Cross from Castleton

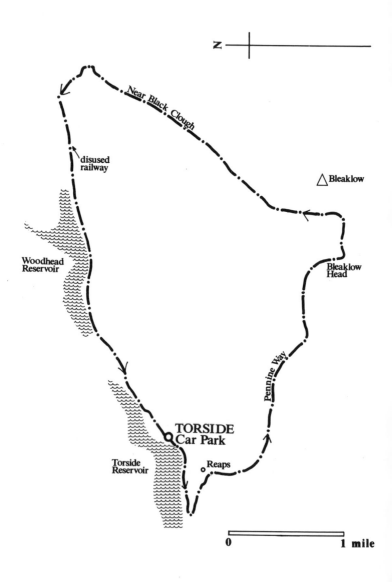

BLEAKLOW

There is a spot on Kinder which is about 15 feet higher than the top of Bleaklow, making Bleaklow the Peak District's K2 to Kinder's Everest. It's still a fine hill, though, and well worth climbing. This walk climbs the hill, then explores Longdendale, where mysterious lights are seen flashing in the sky, and an ancient Celtic religion, supposedly, is still practised.

WALK 1: Torside-Bleaklow-Ironblower

Though there are paths on the ground, it is still easy to lose your way on Bleaklow, so do have a compass with you. This walk starts from the Torside car park on the B6105 from Glossop to Crowden along the south side of Longdendale.

Hard and moderate going, one hard climb.
10 miles, 4 hrs.
Start SK063988.

From the car park go left on to the road and follow it SW for three-quarters of a mile until it crosses the old (disused) railway.

Take the next footpath on the left, signposted as the Pennine Way, through a gate and gently uphill. The path soon bends right, S, and climbs steeply for a short way, after which it climbs more gently for over two miles, swinging E, then SE, then E and finally S once more. If in doubt, simply head for the highest point visible.

When you get there you will see a group of boulders and, to the left, a cairn and a line of stakes stretching across the top of the hill (they're there as waymarkers). Ahead of you and to the right, perched on the edge of the hill, you will be able to see a trig point.

A number of paths meet here. Take the one on the left, which goes E, a little to the left of the line of stakes. After 400 yds it bends left and follows a clough N. Again, if in doubt, retrace your steps to the very top of the hill, near the cairn, and head off on a bearing of 40 degrees. This will bring you to a clough going downhill, almost perfectly straight, NE, with a sort of a path on the left-hand side.

At the bottom (having passed through some trees and on to a broad track) cross the stile and take the footpath on the left, making your way on to the railway, and follow this to the left for two miles, until it meets the road coming from the other side of the valley.

Make your way on to the road (there are a few opportunities) and turn left to return to the car park.

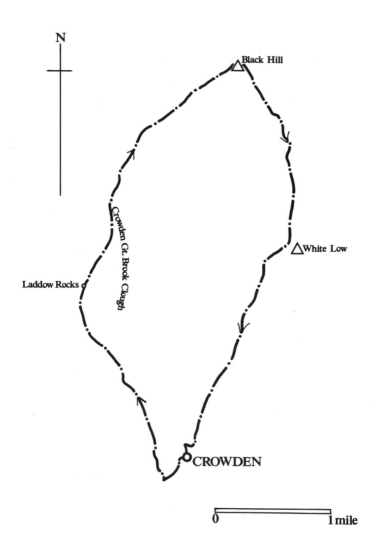

CROWDEN

A walk for fans of Bleakness and Desolation, from lonely Longdendale over the peat hags of Black Hill. Even here, though, there is colour and variety (at certain times of year and in certain places). This walk starts from the car park at Crowden, off the A628 Tintwistle-Penistone road.

WALK 1: Crowden-Black Hill

Moderate and hard going (very hard in wet weather), one long climb.
9 miles, 4 hrs.
Start SK072994.

Take the footpath N out of the car park, making your way along the right side of the camp site until you meet another lane. Turn left and cross Crowden Brook by the bridge. Three hundred yards later, take the signposted footpath on the right (Pennine Way).

This will take you along a narrow path between two walls, to a stile giving on to the open country. Cross over and continue along the footpath along the clough-side.

In spring, and in autumn, this can all look very pleasant – there are isolated pockets of wild flowers. As the path (well-defined) climbs, gently at first, it turns NW, but after a mile it suddenly climbs very sharply up to Laddow Rocks. There is a stream tumbling down the hillside here and, in late summer or autumn when the heather is in bloom, it can look like an ornamental garden.

Follow the top of the cliffs NNE as the clough below you gradually rises to its head. You then find yourself in a broad but shallow peaty valley. Follow the stream (often discoloured) N and NNE until the head of the valley, then climb NE making for the trig point on top of Black Hill.

At the trig point, turn right, heading SSW (there are waymarkings) along the spur of the plateau, keeping the TV mast of Holme Moss to your left. When you can see the lower plateau of White Low below you and slightly right, descend the shoulder between the two hills to the S, past some turf and stone grouse butts.

On White Low, turn half right and descend SW, past a strange mere, to a broad footpath running along this side of the clough and back to Crowden.

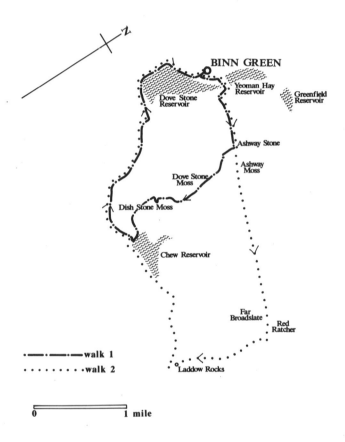

BINN GREEN

Yeoman Hay
Reservoir

Greenfield
Reservoir

Dove Stone
Reservoir

Ashway Stone

Ashway
Moss

Dove Stone
Moss

Dish Stone Moss

Chew Reservoir

Far
Broadslate

Red
Ratcher

Laddow Rocks

•——•——•——• walk 1

• • • • • • • • • walk 2

0   1 mile

SADDLEWORTH MOOR

This is the very north-western fringe of the Peak District, and is closer in character to the mid-Pennine moors than to what we normally associate with the Peak. It's bleak, it's windswept, it's boggy and it's halfway between Holmfirth and Oldham, names redolent of Northern gunge and grime. But it's a wild and beautiful part of the world, and the walking is wonderful – if you don't mind getting wet and muddy.

These walks start from Binn Green, the second car park out of Greenfield (in what is called Greater Manchester but is really Lancashire) on the A635 Oldham-Holmfirth road. As you come out of the town you pass a sign for Dovestones Reservoir, and then the road bends to the north, into rugged moorland. The car park is on the right very soon after the bend, and comes up with very little warning.

WALK 1: Binn Green-Ashway Moss-Chew Clough

A very steep, hard ascent is followed by several miles of windswept bog, and a dramatic descent down a steep, rocky defile. Brilliant!

Moderate-hard going, one long hard climb.
6 miles, 3 hrs.
Start SE018044.

In the car park, turn E and look at the cross set on to the hill-top opposite. You are going up there (just to the right of it). Take the signposted and incredibly glamorous-sounding Oldham Way downhill out of the car park. This brings you to a metalled lane. Turn left following the sign for the open country. Go through a gate and cross the dam between Dovestones Reservoir and Yeoman Hey Reservoir. (We won't even begin to think how it got the name Yeoman Hey, but let's say it in an American accent, wearing our baseball caps the wrong way round and raising a hand in the air. Remarkable, isn't it?)

Follow the path right on the other side and, at the first opportunity, strike left uphill (going due E), heading for Ashway Stone, the biggest of the rocks you can see perched on the brow of the hill. Keep the brook cascading down the hill on your right.

Just below Ashway Stone – you can see the Memorial Cross to your left – take the footpath running off to the right, due S. This brings you to the brook you kept parallel to on the way up and follows it on the left for a little way (past, incidentally, a dry-stone butt which is a very handy place for sandwiching in), and then crosses it via a stone-flagged bridge.

From here things get a little bit harder. There is no path on the ground, and it is very boggy, with groughs getting in your way. You need to follow the clough into which you were led from the footbridge SE for about 400 yds, and then strike off half-right, due S. You should now be going uphill slightly and not encountering too many obstacles.

After about half a mile of this, the ground should start to fall away and you will be looking out from the crest of the moss you are on over a lower one. You will also, if it is not raining too hard, be able to see the tower on the dam of Chew Reservoir. Take a compass bearing on it (it should be close to due S) and follow that bearing (you will lose sight of the tower).

This is where you realise, if you've got any knowledge of the native flora, that the time to come up here is in June. The bogs here are covered in cotton-sedge which, when it's in bloom and not too wet, makes the area look as if it is in snow. Of course, there are only about two days each year when the sedge is out and the sun is shining at the same time, but when they are it is quite spectacular.

At the reservoir, cross the dam on the path. On the other side, take the newly-metalled track leading down the steep-sided Chew Clough. There are, as you descend, all sorts of relics of this valley's industrial past – old quarry workings and the remains of bridges and embankments. One less welcome recent addition is a 'disposal site' near the bottom, but it is not too intrusive. It does make you wonder, though, since the Chew Brook running alongside feeds into the reservoir, about the quality of drinking water in this part of the world.

At the bottom of the clough, take the path on the left, following the edge of Dovestones Reservoir. There will almost undoubtedly be someone sailing on it, even in the dead of winter, possibly on a sailboard. Walk on past the sailing club and turn right, across the dam. On the other side strike uphill and take the footpath which runs to the right on the other side of the small conifer plantation. Where this path splits 500 yds later, take the left fork, signposted back to Binn Green.

WALK 2: Binn Green-Black Chew Head-Laddow-Chew Clough

This is an advanced version of Walk 1, which should only be attempted by those who are confident of their navigational skills – if you're not sure how to use a compass, please don't attempt it. It makes use of the right to roam at will over the access land between Tintwistle and Black Hill but, as a consequence, does not, for a large part of its route, follow any sort of path. I would not recommend anyone doing it in bad visibility.

Hard going, one hard climb.
9 miles, 5 hrs.
Start SE018044.

Follow Walk 1 as far as Ashway Stone. From here take a compass bearing of 115 degrees and bog trot for two miles. This bearing takes you uphill for a little way, close to the top of Featherbed Moss, but then keeps you more or less level.

However, climbing and descending is not your real problem – that is the unfriendliness of the terrain. The sogginess of the ground and the many groughs (great gouges in the peat caused by small streams) make this extremely hard going, and make it easy to lose your way. Keep to that bearing, checking your compass every few yards.

Eventually (on a good day you should be able to do these two miles in 90 minutes, but it may well take longer) you will be able to see the rock formations at the head of Great Crowden Brook Clough. The Pennine Way runs along the top of the steep bit of the slope on this side of the clough, so turn right and follow it for a mile.

There are, by the way, some extraordinarily fearless and even aggressive sheep here which have, it seems, become inured to the natural threat posed by humans because of the huge numbers of walkers doing the Way. Do your bit to counteract this by shouting Boo! at one of them. The rocky ridge here is, potentially, a great place to Cornish pasty and tomato soup, but your lunch can be spoiled by inquisitive ovines.

One mile later the Pennine Way takes a left bend and heads steeply downhill. This is a beautiful spot. There is a small waterfall, and in August and September when the heathers are in bloom it looks like a rock-garden, being especially beautiful against the red of the dying bracken.

Here turn right on a track which leads uphill and slightly back on the way you have come. This track is quite clearly defined, and heads north-west for three-quarters of a mile, then west to the dam at the west end of Chew Reservoir. From the reservoir follow Walk 1 back to base.

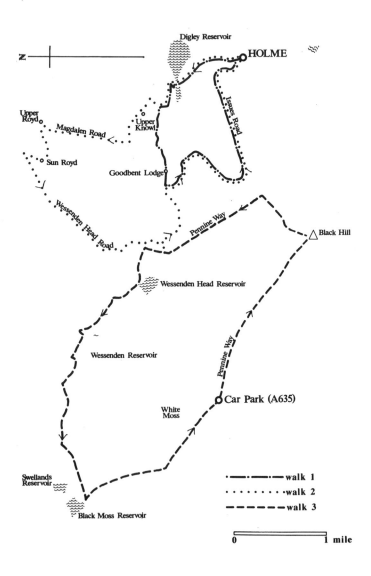

N

Digley Reservoir

HOLME

Issues Road

Upper
Royd

Magdalen Road

Upper
Knowl

Sun Royd

Goodbent Lodge

Wessenden Head Road

Pennine Way

Black Hill

Wessenden Head Reservoir

Wessenden Reservoir

Pennine Way

Car Park (A635)

White
Moss

Swellands
Reservoir

Black Moss Reservoir

—·—·—·— walk 1
· · · · · · · · · walk 2
— — — — walk 3

0   1 mile

WESSENDEN

The most northerly, and in many ways the bleakest of the Peak's moors, perhaps because the countryside here has far more in common with the Pennine Moors which stretch from here far into Yorkshire and beyond than with the rest of the Peak further south. Wessenden is nevertheless great walking country, much of it being open access. Two of these walks start from the village of Holme on the A6024 Holmfirth road – there is car parking off the road north of the Fleece Inn. Walk 3 starts from the car park on the A635 Oldham-Holmfirth road, 30 yds east of the old Lancashire border.

WALK 1: Holme-Bradshaw

A short, easy walk surrounded by dramatic hills.

Easy and moderate going, one short climb.
5 miles, 2 hrs.
Start SE108060.

Start in the broad, cobbled square, north of the Fleece, on the western side of the main road (where the bus to Holmfirth departs from). Take the lane which forks off to the right. A few hundred yards later, the lane bends left and there is a large, low, stone barn on the right-hand side (it has a narrow green door). Immediately to the left of this, take the signposted footpath on the right.

This heads downhill, going more or less N across fields, for about 500 yds before bending slightly W and running uphill from, but parallel to, the S bank of Digley Reservoir.

Where the reservoir narrows and comes to an end, bend right with the path and follow it to the other side of the valley and uphill slightly to meet a lane. Turn left and follow this lane as it bends right (N) to meet a second lane, bounded by dry-stone walls. This is Bradshaw, a loose, spread-out settlement which shows all the signs of having once been more heavily populated than it is today.

Turn left again and follow this lane due W (though it twists and turns somewhat) for almost a mile, as, after a right bend, it starts to climb. You pass two farm buildings on your left. Four hundred yards after the second, but well before the lane takes a second, more serious right, cross the stile and take the footpath on your left downhill into the bottom of the clough.

The path continues on the other side climbing SE and then, gradually, turning right through 90 degrees as it climbs over a spur of the moor and into the next clough. You should cross the stream in this clough and climb the opposite bank for a short way until, looking down to your left, you can see a lane running between fields and heading ENE, towards Holmfirth.

Make for the lane and follow it for almost a mile, past a junction on the right, until it meets another. Turn right and follow this downhill into Holme.

WALK 2: Holme-Bradshaw-Meltham Moor

A more strenuous walk venturing over the spectacularly craggy ground (rich in prehistoric sites) south of the mill town of Meltham.

Moderate, occasionally hard, going with one major climb.
9 miles, 4 hrs.
Start SE108060.

Follow Walk 1 to the lane past Digley Reservoir. Turn left on to the lane and follow it as it bends N to meet another. Here, cross the stile opposite and take the footpath which climbs, in effect (though it does some bending), due N to enter another lane to the right of a farm.

Crossing the stile here, take the lane opposite leading NW to the major road. At the road turn left, taking the next footpath on the right after 300 yds. This path heads downhill on a bearing of eight degrees to meet a lane to the left of a farm.

Follow this lane round to the right for 250 yds, then take the lane to the left which heads downhill, past another farm building, to the bottom of the clough and crosses it, heading due W, to the left of a clump of trees.

Climbing up the other side it meets another lane at a farm, running NNE along the top of the steep edge of the clough. Turn right into this and follow it for 500 yds until it starts to bend right. Take the footpath on the left here, past traces of a prehistoric settlement (there is nothing much to see) and climb the shoulder of the clough heading ESE. The last bit of the climb is quite steep and brings you out on to a minor road, at which point turn left.

Follow this road for a mile-and-a-half, pausing, perhaps (but probably not), to see if there's anyone crowing on the Cock Crowing Stone (you can tell which it is because it has 'Cock Crowing Stone' written on it) and probably making the brief detour to climb to the trig point at West Nab for the view of glorious Huddersfield.

At the main road take the footpath opposite. There is a path on the ground and it leads downhill SSE towards the bottom of a clough and gradually bends ENE, keeping its height once the clough starts to broaden out. Keeping left of a small clump of trees will bring you to the corner of a lane.

Turn right where the lane forks and take the next footpath on the right, down to the bottom of the clough and over the other side, heading SE and then, gradually, turning right through 90 degrees as it climbs over a spur of the moor and into the next clough. You should cross the stream in this clough and climb the opposite bank for a short way until, looking down to your left, you can see a lane running between fields and heading ENE, towards Holmfirth.

Make for the lane and follow it for almost a mile, past a junction on the right, until it meets another. Turn right and follow this downhill into Holme.

WALK 3: Wessenden car park-Black Hill-Wessenden-Black Moss

This walk involves traversing difficult country often with few landmarks or distinguishing features, so a compass really is a must. It is also not a terribly good idea to venture on to the high moors in this area in bad visibility.

Hard going, two hard climbs.
9 miles, 4½ hrs.
Start SE051064.

From the car park cross the road and the stile on to the footpath marked as the Pennine Way. There is little in the way of a path on the ground, though it is staked. It heads straight up Black Hill on a bearing of 123 degrees. (It's two miles, though it is impossble to tell how far you've walked in country like this.)

Make for the trig point at the top of Black Hill, where there is a bit of a view in all directions. See if you can find the path leading away NNE into a clough – it is marked with cairns but there are times when it appears indistinct – and if so follow it into the clough for half a mile until it bends left, heading NNE to the road. It is, again, marked but, if at any point you lose your way, a bearing of a few degrees W of N will bring you to the road. If you can't find the path, follow a bearing of 357 degrees to the road.

Either of these routes should bring you to the A635 at the Meltham turn-off. Take the Meltham road and then the footpath on the left down a broad track leading to the Wessenden Head reservoir. Follow it down to the dam at the NW end of the reservoir, then strike off NW, keeping to the right-hand side of the valley.

After three-quarters of a mile, keep to the side of the next reservoir. After the dam, take the track on the left parallel to the brook, then, where it bends right (N) cross the brook and head up the northernmost of the two cloughs on the other side. You should be heading roughly E.

Climb this as it bends round to the left slightly and you find yourself looking down on yet another reservoir. A heading of roughly 250 degrees should then bring you to a fourth and final reservoir, at the SE corner of which is a distinct track (the Pennine Way) leading SSE back to the car park (two miles). Should you fancy more cross-country orienteering, the exact bearing on the car park is 143 degrees.

Woods by Oxlow Rake (Peak Forest)

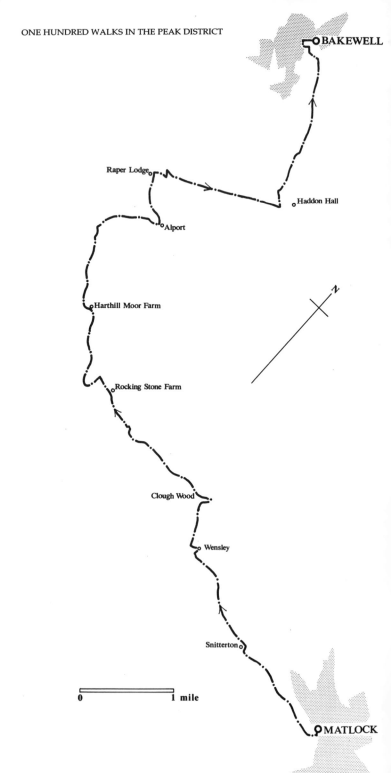

RIBBON WALKS

MATLOCK-BAKEWELL

A reasonably gentle walk over some delightful limestone countryside, including sections of riverside walking, with many features of interest along the way.

Buses between Matlock and Bakewell (principally the R1 and 32) are relatively frequent so basing yourself in Bakewell and catching a bus to the start, or in Matlock and bussing back to Matlock (where there is a railway station) are equally feasible.

Easy and moderate going, steep climbs early on.
11½ miles, 5 hrs.
Start SK298603.

In Matlock, come out of the bus station on to Bakewell Road and turn left, taking the next right over the bridge. On the other side take Snitterton Road, first right past the entrance to the railway station.

Follow this for a mile, between two quarries, to a sharp right bend at the entrance to Snitterton Hall. At the second of the two driveways, take the footpath on the left heading NNW for 50 yds before bending left at a wall.

This well-defined path leads you, half a mile later, into the bottom of Wensley Dale. Walking along the track at the bottom of the dale, look for the rows of houses above you to the right. Where a narrow path comes diagonally down the hillside from the left, take one of the footpaths on the right and climb up into the village. Turn left on the main street.

Walk through the village, past the pub. Just past the last house on the right, take the footpath on the right, uphill – the little circular ponds, by the way, are old flooded mineshafts. Over the top this descends, steeply and prettily, into some woods. At the bottom, cross the scrubby bottom of the valley and take the path on the right, on to a broad, stony path on the left which zigzags up the hillside.

At the top of the path turn left and pass in front of a strange derelict arch and back into woods. There now follows a long, and if it is a hot summer's day, sticky, climb, but the woods are very pleasant, especially when the honeysuckle is in flower.

You will eventually find yourself climbing a clough, which takes you out of the trees and through a field, on to a pleasant lane. Turn left and follow the lane on to an open hilltop, looking down left on to Winster and right on to Birchover. Follow this for half a mile, bending around some farmhouses to come out on to a minor road.

Turn left to pass in front of the cottages opposite and take the footpath on the right immediately after. It runs along the uphill side of some woods before bending right and left on to a lane and passing left of the very pretty Rocking Stone Farm. Carry on past the hillock behind the farm, turning sharp left to cross three long fields and emerge on a main road.

Cross this and cut across the field opposite (via the footpath) on to a narrow lane and turn right. This comes downhill to meet the road 300 yds later, but on its final left bend take the footpath straight on, which bends left and heads uphill to the left of some trees.

On the top of the hill this passes right of Robin Hood's Stride, a natural rock formation (an outcrop of gritstone which has eroded more slowly than the surrounding limestone). In the woods below this to the right is a hermit's cave, complete with bench and niche carved into the rock (there's a footpath leading to it), and the top of this moor is also covered with neolithic and bronze-age sites.

The footpath crosses a road and passes left of a farm, heading NW, downhill, towards Youlgreave for almost two miles. It comes out on to a road on the outskirts of the village. Turn right and follow the road across the River Bradford, taking the footpath immediately on the right, along the river bank. It crosses a footbridge soon after and follows the right bank for half a mile.

This brings you, past some interesting limestone formations on your right, including a cleft rock, into the tiny village of Alport. Cross the road and head up the grassy area opposite, into Lathkill Dale. There is no path on the ground, but follow the left side of the wall running parallel to the river. There are stiles to aim for.

After half a mile of this you pass in front of Raper Lodge and on to a lane. Turn right and cross the river on to a steep, zigzagging path up the other bank of the dale. Once back on relatively level ground, head left of the mine workings on the well-defined footpath heading ENE across fields. A mile later, this descends on to the A6 by the car park for Haddon Hall. Turn left.

Two-hundred-and-fifty yards later, take the footpath on the right (it can be obscured by overgrowth, so look for it carefully). It crosses the River Wye, and follows its right bank for a further mile, into Bakewell. After crossing the showground it is probably best to turn left and cross the footbridge into the town centre.

Conies Dale (Peak Forest)

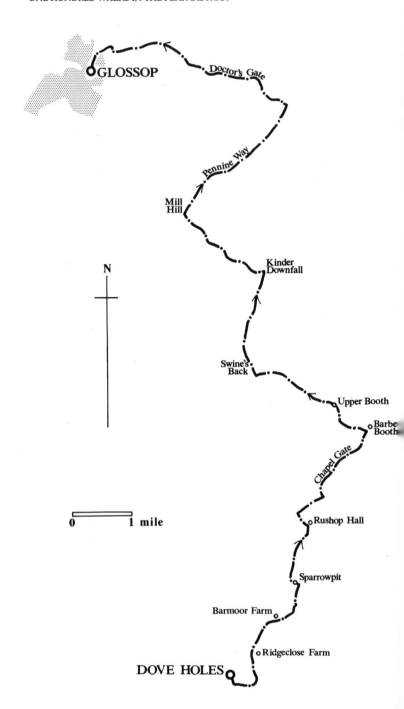

DOVE HOLES-GLOSSOP

The longest walk in the book, and amongst the hardest, this is a marathon (almost) which should only be undertaken by the experienced and hardy.

Dove Holes station is on the Manchester-Buxton line, Glossop on the Manchester-Hadfield line, so parking a car at one end and returning via train requires a bit of pre-planning. It might be better, therefore, to base yourself in Manchester to do this one.

Hard and moderate going, one very hard climb.
19 miles, 8 hrs.
Start SK074782.

From Dove Holes Station head E into the village to the main road. Not a promising start to a walk, admittedly, but it gets better. Take the road signposted to Smalldale. Just behind those houses on the left is the Bull Henge, one of the largest and most important prehistoric sites in the North of England. There's not that much to see, though.

After 350 yds, take the signposted footpath on the left, between a clump of trees and the quarry workings on your right. Follow this N for half a mile. Where the track starts to bend left, keep to your former heading as far as possible, crossing a farm lane and bending slightly right to head uphill over a field to another lane.

Now join a farm lane heading NE along the side of the valley, keeping right of a series of farms, and keeping parallel to the road below you. This brings you out on to the main road where it bends E from Sparrowpit. Turn left.

Opposite the Wanted Inn in Sparrowpit, take the signposted footpath on the corner of the Bagshaw road. This heads due N before bending NNE and hugging the contours of the hill, coming to the Rushup-Perryfoot road a mile later.

Turn left on the road and follow it uphill to the main road. Turn right here and shortly after take the footpath on the left. Keep left of the wall, in that strange rut. Six hundred yards later take the footpath on the left, going right and downhill on the broad, defined track at the cairn 300 yds later.

Follow this downhill to the road at Barber Booth and turn left. Go under the railway bridge, round a right and left bend and past the houses at Upper Booth (sometimes known as Telephone Booth for its isolated phone box). Go through the gate on to the valley lane ENE to Lee Farm.

This continues pleasantly for a mile. Then the track comes to an old packhorse bridge. Cross this, turning to the left and start the long steep climb up Jacob's Ladder.

After the climb has eased off, you come to a wall where the path forks. Go right (NNE) with the Pennine Way, still climbing. Here the path on the ground bends around to the right, but you need to keep heading NNE and keep climbing, over Kinder Low, the highest point in the Peak District. There are cairns to mark the way, and the trig point is a useful point of reference if you can see it.

You will then come to the western perimeter of Kinder. Follow it. There's no path, but it is easy to find your way as you simply have to keep the sharp drop to your left. A mile of this and you come to Kinder Downfall, where the River Kinder sometimes falls over the edge of the plateau. (Sometimes it doesn't, depends on the weather.)

The edge here takes a severe left turn and you are now heading WNW. Follow this another mile-and-a-half as you descend into a broad, boggy, shallow valley. Go up the other side, heading NW, on what is now a clear path. At the top of this hill turn right, following the footpath and line of stakes leading NNE along the ridge for two-and-a-half miles until it crosses the usually busy Snake Road between Manchester and Sheffield. (Should it happen that you can't see your way here, head NE and lose as little height as possible.)

Four hundred yards after crossing the Snake Road, nip down into the Doctor's Gate cutting and take this well-marked path to the left. It descends into a clough and follows this downhill for the next two miles, coming to the boundary of the open country above Glossop.

Continue on the path, passing a farm and a reservoir on your left, as it gradually bends left and becomes a semi-metalled lane. This comes out on to a road opposite a factory. Carry straight on, past the factory and into Old Glossop. Four hundred yards later is the T-junction with Manor Park Road. Turn left, then right at the main road and the station is 600 yds further, right again after the traffic lights.

Below Hollins Cross (Castleton)

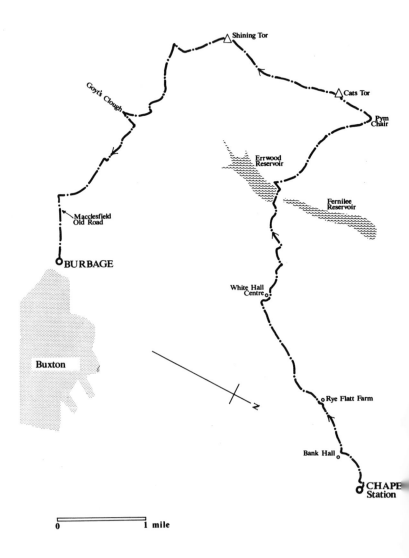

CHAPEL-BUXTON

A ten-minute train ride and this walk enables you to wander the wild moors between two of the Peak's bigger towns. The walk covers a variety of moorland and valley scenery, and includes a climb up Shining Tor, the highest hill in this part of the Peak.

> *Chapel-en-le-Frith and Buxton are on the same railway line, so this is an easy one to organise – especially if you make the outward journey by train from Buxton so you don't have to try to co-ordinate your walking with the BR timetable.*

Moderate and hard going, three climbs.
11 miles, 5 hrs.
Start SK055795.

Assuming you have come from Buxton by train, cross the footbridge and take the narrow lane on the left for 200 yds, turning left again to pass under the railway. Emerging on the other side, take the footpath immediately on the right, over a stile and then heading SSW over rough pasture, hugging the wall to the left and climbing gently for half a mile before descending to a minor road.

Go right for 100 yds, taking the farm lane (signposted as a footpath) on the left through the farmyard, bending left towards another farm some 400 yds later. Once past the entrance to this, the lane peters out, but there is a path on the ground which crosses a stream and heads roughly SW across the hillside, climbing, to emerge on a lane by the White Hall Mountain Rescue Post and activity centre.

Turn right on the lane, passing the buildings on your left. Go straight over at the crossroads, taking the footpath on the right as the lane is bending right 200 yds later. This footpath climbs over the hill and descends the other side, crossing the often busy Buxton-Whaley Bridge road on to a track, which bends left 150 yds later to meet another.

Carry straight on to a stile in the bottom right corner of the field and follow the wall around to the bottom of the valley, making your way up the other side a little way to meet a minor road. Turn right and follow this across the Errwood Dam.

On the other side follow the road around to the left to a T-junction. Turn right and follow this for a mile-and-a-half to the car park at Pym Chair – the top of the hill, where the Tors ridge climbs up to your left and the road descends sharply in front of you affording a spectacular view of Macclesfield.

Take the footpath on the left and follow the ridge for two miles. At the trig point on top of Shining Tor, the path bends left and descends sharply (climbing a little after this) to pass through a gap in a stone wall and meet another footpath. Turn right and squish your way along what can be one of the boggiest stretches of path known to man, to climb a stile over a high stone wall.

On the other side take the footpath on the left, downhill, for a mile. It crosses a clough and follows the perimeter of a plantation for a while before entering it.

Where the path emerges from the trees, near the bottom, follow it around to the right and make your way down to the road. Turn left and take the next (signposted) footpath on the right, crossing the footbridge and taking the footpath steeply up the clough.

Follow this to the top of the hill, until you come to a wood, then follow it to the right, to a lane – Macclesfield Old Road. Turn left and follow this into the outskirts of Buxton (Burbage). Half a mile later you come to the main road. Turn left. Buses into Buxton (X23 or 188) can be caught from outside the church (but not terribly often), or you can walk back to the centre of town by simply following the main road (one mile).

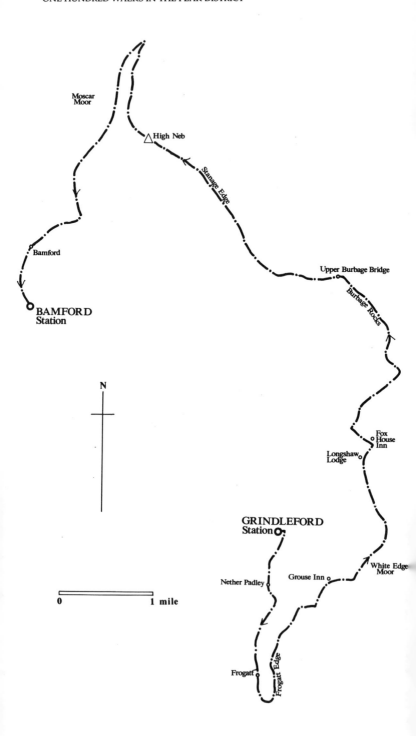

GRINDLEFORD-BAMFORD

A walk which starts out through ancient woodlands and then follows the dramatic and rocky eastern edge which, especially to the south, marks the limit of the wild gritstone moorland as it encroaches on the lusher limestone.

The walk starts from Grindleford Station (typically, this is not in Grindleford, it's in Nether Padley) and finishes at Bamford Station, which are both on the Hope Valley line, making it perfectly feasible to park a car at either of the stations and make the train journey to Grindleford either before or after the walk. Alternatively, the line runs between Manchester and Sheffield, making it quite possible to do the whole thing by public transport.

Moderate going, one hard climb.
15 miles, 6 hrs.
Start SK250789.

Take the station lane SSW on to the main road and turn right. Follow the road around a gentle left bend and, shortly after a lane off to the left, take the footpath on the left to Froggatt. This heads for the right-hand side of the woods before bending left into them and resuming its former course.

After a mile the path emerges through a wooden gate and on to a minor road. Turn left, uphill, on to the main road, and turn right. Follow this for 600 yds, passing the Chequers Inn on your left and, immediately after, taking the footpath on the left. This climbs steeply uphill through the woods to Froggat Edge, turning sharply right to get on top of the edge once out of the trees.

On the edge, head N-ish (i.e. turn left), and follow the path along the top as it bends around to the right for almost a mile. It comes out on to a bend in the road. Turn right and follow it past the Grouse Inn on your left, taking the footpath on the right immediately after it, on to open country.

After 400 yds turn left and follow the line of rocks NE, keeping right of the clumps of trees at the far end, after which head due N to emerge over a stile on to the road at a junction.

Take the road opposite (signposted to Hathersage) and the footpath on the left 50 yds later. This heads downhill and comes to the perimeter of some woods. Follow the perimeter right and back up to the road. Turn left to a T-junction opposite Fox House Inn and turn left.

After 500 yds, take the first footpath on the right, climbing uphill to follow the top of Burbage Rocks NE, then swinging left as they run NNW to a minor road almost a mile later.

Turn left on to the road, cross the small bridge over the Burbage Brook and, where the road bends left, take the broad path straight on to a trig point at the end of Stanage Edge.

Follow the path along the top of Stanage Edge for four miles, until you run out of edge and start descending. Here, turn back on yourself and make due S, under the edge, for the middle of the shoulder between the edge and the hill opposite.

Climb the hill to your right, descending again down the spur which protrudes S. This will bring you to a stile giving on to a road. Turn right and follow the road for 150 yds, taking the overgrown lane on the left as the road bends right.

This takes you steeply downhill SW into the village. Turn left on the main road for the railway station (three-quarters of a mile).

Climbing to Hollins Cross from Castleton

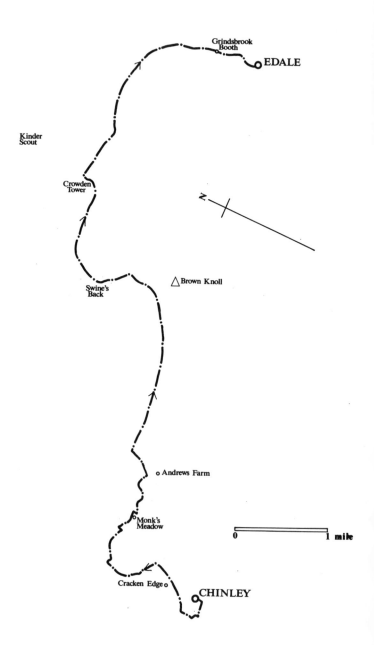

CHINLEY-EDALE

A walk which is really one long climb on to Kinder Scout, followed by a rapid and dramatic descent into Edale, this is relatively short, but quite taxing.

Chinley and Edale are both on the Manchester-Sheffield via Hope Valley line, so the walk can be done by car users and by those relying solely on public transport.

Hard and moderate going, one long climb, one shorter.
9½ miles, 4 hrs.
Start SK038826.

From Chinley Station make your way down Station Road, past the new houses and on to the village main road. Turn right. Three hundred yards along the road turn right through the white wooden gate, over the railway bridge and on to the footpath going up the right side of the paddock to a minor road.

Turn left and follow the road round a right bend, immediately afterwards taking the lane on the right. Follow this uphill and as it bends left half a mile later, take the footpath on the right once on open pasture.

This will take you N along the top of the hill, passing woods below you and right. As soon as the woods finish, take the footpath on the right and descend steeply. You are going over the main road on the other side of the valley and up the big hill in front of you and slightly left.

At a minor road, turn left and take the first right, continuing down to the bottom of the valley and up to the road on the other side. You emerge almost opposite the Lamb Inn. Just to the right of it, take the signposted (though the sign gets hidden by vegetation) footpath on the left uphill from the grassy verge.

After three fields, this path meets another. Turn left and head NE, coming to a stile and the boundary of open country. Cross over and follow the footpath on the right, heading due E. Follow this path (it's quite distinct) for two miles, climbing the long shoulder of Brown Knoll, and gradually turning northwards.

A few hundred yards after starting to descend northwards, you meet a path coming from the right with, very often, quite a lot of red-faced, knackered people on it. They have just come up Jacob's Ladder (one of the most arduous climbs in the Peak). Remark in a loud voice that the last time you came up Jacob's Ladder you were with your 80-year-old grandmother, who found it no trouble at all and you don't know what all the fuss is about.

Carry straight on along the well-defined path, joining the

Pennine Way for a short while, bending round to the right and climbing on to the southern edge of the Kinder Scout plateau.

Once on the high edge of the plateau, and looking down to the right into a steep-sided valley, head E for half a mile, until you cross the top of a spur of the plateau sticking out below you. The path here bends left slightly, going NE for a few hundred yards before reaching the edge again and resuming its eastwards course once it has rounded the head of a clough falling away SSE.

A further three-quarters of a mile of heading E will take you over another spur to the edge of Grindsbrook Clough. Make your way down this, still heading E – there is a path, but it can be a bit slippery. The path keeps more or less to the bottom of the clough as it bends around to the right and ends up heading SSE.

You will then, after a mile of this, come to a stile. The footpath on the other side leads through some trees to Edale, bending right to cross the brook half a mile after the stile. There are two pubs between you and the railway station, the Nag's Head and the Rambler's Inn. Guess which one is more walker-friendly? (Yup, the Nag.)

Woods by Oxlow Rake (Peak Forest)

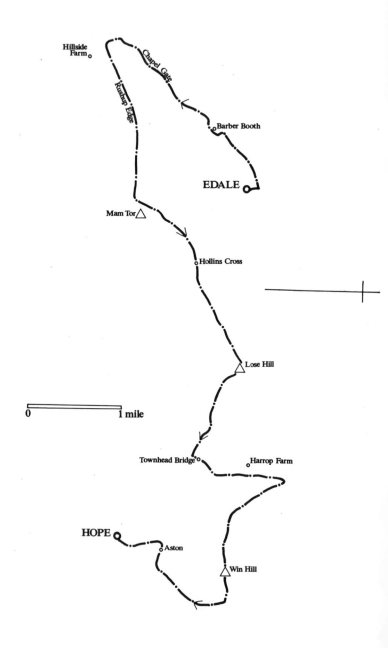

EDALE-HOPE

This is the Peak's ridge-walk par excellence – the four hills in a row, Lord's Seat, Mam Tor, Lose Hill and Win Hill are all scaled. The immediate surroundings may not change all that much, but the views are spectacular. Edale and Hope are on the same railway line.

Moderate going, two long climbs.
12½ miles, 5½ hrs.
Start SK124853.

Come out of the station and turn left into Edale. Take the first footpath on the left (clearly signposted to Barber Booth) after the Rambler's Inn. This follows a lane for a while, then heads across fields and a bridge over the railway before turning left on to the valley road at Barber Booth.

On the road turn right, then take the next turning right, signposted to Upper Booth. Two hundred yards along this road, take the signposted footpath on the left climbing gently over fields to the right of a farm. It then joins a well-defined track – Chapel Gate, the old Edale-Chapel-en-le-Frith packhorse route.

This climbs quite severely SW on to open moorland. At the top of the steep bit of the climb it crosses a wall and bends left, to head more directly S. Where it meets the next wall, join the track running along your side of it and turn left.

Follow the ridge – Rushup Edge – for the next mile-and-a-half as it rises over Lord's Seat, the highest point, and dips down towards Mam Tor.

Coming out on to the road, take the footpath opposite and to the right, straight to the top of the hill. Pause at the trig point for a look around, then continue along the ridge for another two miles, until it finishes. This involves some climbing, especially as you climb Lose Hill (pronounced 'loose hill'), the steep little pimple at the very end. The view from here, however, is terrific.

From the cairn on top of Lose Hill, turn right and take the footpath running straight downhill. After you have crossed a stone wall, look for and take the path which bears left slightly, to take you ESE. This leads down to Hope Townhead. As the descent is easing off it joins a farm lane. Keep heading in more or less the same direction and you will come out on to a bend in Edale Road. Turn left on the road and cross the bridge over the River Noe, taking the lane opposite when the road bends left.

This lane crosses over the railway and starts to climb, turning left at a farm and climbing more steeply, but very prettily, on to the open moorside.

When you are in open pasture, the path forks. Head slightly to the right, uphill. At the crest of the shoulder of the hill, turn right again, taking the broad path which you can see climbing the shoulder.

Follow the path as it bends left and climbs to the very top of Win Hill Pike, the rocky little outcrop at the end. Take the footpath down the other side of Win Hill Pike, passing through a gate stile when you come to a stone wall, and heading down into the plantation. Here you need to turn right at the first opportunity, keeping your height and following the left side of a wall for 400 yds before striking off right (uphill for a little way) and making your way, across fields, downhill to Aston.

This will bring you on to a minor road by some houses. Turn right and follow the road through the village (though, in truth, Aston is little more than a very loose string of houses), past a left turn and around a long, sweeping left bend. Where this bend reverses and goes right, take the footpath on the left, which leads across fields to Hope Station.

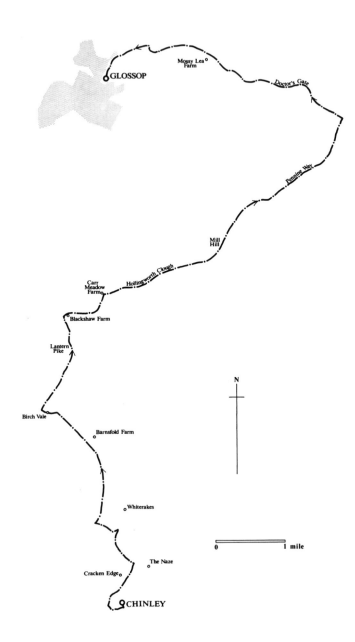

CHINLEY-GLOSSOP

Skirting the western edge of the Peak, this walk starts off in suburban territory and ends up crossing some wild, desolate and strikingly beautiful moorland. It is very taxing.

Note that Chinley and Glossop are not on the same railway line, so, if using public transport, this walk should be based in Manchester.

Hard and moderate going, three hard climbs.
15 miles, 7 hrs.
Start SK038826.

From Chinley Station make your way down Station Road, past the new houses and on to the village main road. Turn right. Three hundred yards along the road turn right through the white wooden gate, over the railway bridge and on to the footpath going up the right side of the paddock to a minor road.

Turn left and follow the road round a right bend, immediately afterwards taking the lane on the right. Follow this uphill and as it bends left half a mile later, taking the footpath on the right once on open pasture.

After 500 yds, make your way left over stiles to a broad footpath running NE alongside a wall just over the brow of the hill. Follow this as it bends N and takes you downhill into Birch Vale, emerging beside the Grouse Inn.

Cross the road and head up the road opposite (Station Road, though the station has long since gone west – you'll pass its mortal remains a little way down on the right).

Passing a cafe in a shack on your left, and crossing the River Sett, you'll come to a row of posh cottages on the right called the Crescent. Immediately after these, take the steep, cobbled lane on the right. Follow this uphill to a row of five rather less posh cottages at Windy Knoll, and take the lane opposite and to the right. Continue in the same direction as before, still climbing.

Pass in front of a house and, as the lane narrows to a path, you will find yourself on open moorland and passing into the National Trust property on top of Lantern Pike. It's worth nipping up to the top of the hill for the view and the hell of it, but the path keeps close to the left-hand side of the stone wall.

Coming down the other side, the path bends right across a field and comes to a meeting of ways at a signpost. Turn right and follow the footpath to Carr Meadow. Skirt Blackshaw Farm to the left, continuing in the same direction as before and making your way down to the main road on a farm lane.

Turn left on the road (this is probably the most dangerous bit of the walk – do be careful) and follow it for 400 yds, past some houses on the left, to a left bend. Cross over the stile on the right at the apex of this bend into open country. You are in a broad clough (Hollingworth Clough) and must now follow it to its head.

For the first mile-and-a-half it is easy to follow, but, as a general guide, try to make sure you are always heading either E or ENE. At the head of the clough keep climbing, though head NE. This will bring you to the top of Mill Hill, well over a thousand feet higher than the road you recently left.

From the top of the hill a footpath and a line of stakes leads away NNE along the ridge. This is the Pennine Way. Follow it for two-and-a-half miles until it crosses the usually busy Snake Road between Manchster and Sheffield. (Should it happen that you can't see your way here, head NE and lose as little height as possible.)

Four hundred yards after crossing the Snake Road, nip down into the Doctor's Gate cutting and take the well-marked path on the left. It descends into a clough and follows this downhill for the next two miles, coming to the boundary of the open country above Glossop.

Continue on the path, passing a farm and a reservoir on your left, as it gradually bends left and becomes a semi-metalled lane. This comes out on to a road opposite a factory. Carry straight on, past the factory and into Old Glossop. Four hundred yds later is the T-junction with Manor Park Road. Turn left, and then right at the main road and the station is 600 yds further (right after the traffic lights).

Conies Dale (Peak Forest)

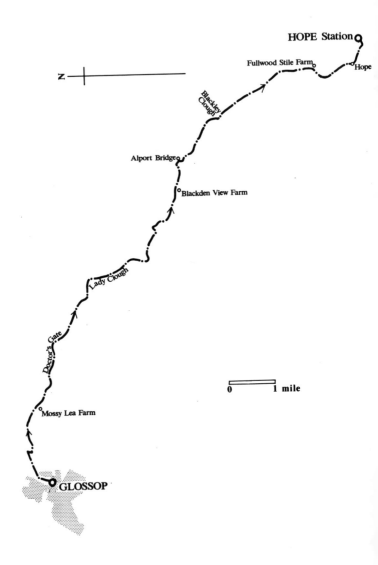

GLOSSOP-HOPE

This walk follows the Roman road which ran from Glossop to the fort at Navio (Brough). It climbs through the spectacular scenery between Bleaklow and Kinder Scout, before entering the bottom of the Vale of Edale and the Hope Valley. It can be done by people entirely reliant on public transport – it starts at Glossop Station and ends at Hope Station, so you can do it from either Sheffield or Manchester. Though the last trains from Hope run quite late (11ish) in both directions, it would be an idea to check on the precise times beforehand as the service is not frequent.

Moderate going, one long climb at the beginning.
14 miles, 7 hrs.
Start SK034943.

Come out of Glossop Station on to Norfolk Street and turn right, past the Howard, to the traffic lights. Turn left into High St East and follow it for 600 yds then turn left up Manor Park Road into the much prettier Old Glossop. After another 800 yds take the first turning on the right (before the church) and follow this past a factory to its end.

Past the bus-turning area and to the right is the entrance to a farm lane (a sign says No Vehicular Access, but it's alright – you're on foot and it's a right of way). Go down it. You are now on the Roman road. Try walking like a Roman.

Stay on this lane until you reach the boundary of the open country, and then take the footpath branching off to the right. This leads SE a little way before turning due E along the bottom of a clough.

You will emerge two-and-a-half miles later on the Snake Road at practically its highest point. Turn left, taking advantage of the wide verge to avoid walking on the road. At the end of the next clough, 500 yds down the road, cross the road and nip over the railings, making your way down to the bottom of Lady Clough, which runs parallel to the road.

Follow the clough round as it bends right, and enter the Forestry Commission plantation by the stile. The footpath follows the bottom of the clough through the plantation for a mile-and-a-half, eventually coming to the other end and a footbridge over the stream to your right. Take the footpath on the left here, bringing you back on to the Snake Road.

Take the Forestry Commission path opposite and to the left which heads due E and brings you back to the Roman road after 400 yds. Turn right and follow it out of the woods.

The path runs roughly parallel to the Snake Road for almost two miles, before dropping down through a farmyard close to the road.

Here take the lane on the left, away from the road, for 300 yds, then fork right to meet the road at Alport Bridge.

Cross the road and take the lane opposite, crossing the river and bending left towards Upper Ashop. At the boundary of the open country, bend left with the lane and climb slightly. The lane skirts the foot of Kinder, bending gradually around to the right before leaving the open country and starting to climb the north-western spur of Win Hill. If it's starting to get dark here, instead of trying to walk like a Roman, you could try Roman in the Gloamin'.

Having climbed some way up Win Hill, and being able to see the railway line below you and the distinctive shape of Lose Hill to your right, the lane begins to descend again, bending right and heading due S.

At Fulwood Stile Farm the lane bends sharply right and crosses the railway. Joining Edale Road, turn left. A few hundred yards on your right is the Cheshire Cheese, a magnificent pub. You deserve a pint or two.

Suitably refreshed (the Cheese stays open all day) carry on along Edale Road to the heart of Hope, turning left on to the main road opposite the church. The turning on the left to the station is 600 yds further on.